Praise for
FATHER and SON

"... a vibrant picture of early 20th-century life [that] will appeal to readers who appreciate stories of immigration, war, family bonds, and the search for identity.... a heartfelt narrative that honors memory while confronting history."
—Carol Thompson for *Readers' Favorite*

"... a powerful and poignant narrative ... skillfully blending historical context with raw emotion ... detailed with a sincere humility to it.... a unique perspective on the delicate balance between familial loyalty and personal identity, making this book a thoughtful read that leans into ideology, family, and national loyalty."
—Asher Syed for *Readers' Favorite*

"... an absolutely fascinating book.... Rudy Jensen writes with feeling, compassion, and honesty. He made me feel like I was there with him as he defended his country. And, although his interactions with his father were often heartbreaking, they provide an in-depth look at a situation that others also must have gone through. I highly recommend this excellent book."
—Joe Wisinski for *Readers' Favorite*

FATHER *and* SON

FATHER *and* SON

The Hitler Loyalist *and the* US Airman

★★★★★★★★★

A Memoir by
RUDY JENSEN
with
MARY K. JENSEN

ASTORIA BOOKS

Copyright © 2025, Rudy Jensen

All rights reserved. No part of this publication may be reproduced, distributed, or transmitted in any form or by any means, including photocopying, recording, digital scanning, or other electronic or mechanical methods, without the prior written permission of the publisher, except in the case of brief quotations embodied in critical reviews and certain other noncommercial uses permitted by copyright law. For permission requests, please address Astoria Books.

Published 2025
Printed in the United States of America
Paperback ISBN: 978-1-7364605-8-0
E-ISBN: 978-1-7364605-9-7

Astoria Books
Seattle, WA
info@astoriabooks.com

Editing and book design by Stacey Aaronson, www.thebookdoctorisin.com
Photos reproduced by David York, dyorkdesign@comcast.net

NO AI TRAINING: Without in any way limiting the author's [and publisher's] exclusive rights under copyright, any use of this publication to "train" generative artificial intelligence (AI) technologies to generate text is expressly prohibited. The author reserves all rights to license uses of this work for generative AI training and development of machine learning language models.

This book is a memoir that reflects the author's recollections of experiences over time. The events, places, and conversations have been recreated from memory, and in some instances, details have been changed, altered, or compressed for the purposes of narrative flow. Names and identifying characteristics of some individuals have been changed or omitted to protect their privacy and anonymity. The author has made every effort to be factually accurate, but the nature of memory means some details may be imperfect.

*To those who lost their lives in the Kassel Mission
and to those who today keep alive their memory*

table of contents

The Backstory ... 1
1 The Lucky Guys ... 3
2 Waiting ... 7
3 Papa: A First Look ... 10
4 My First Mother ... 13
5 My First Voyage ... 16
6 Loss ... 21
7 Four-Year-Old Sailor ... 26
8 A New Mother ... 31
9 Fitting in ... 36
10 Prohibition and the Family ... 40
11 Another Look *at* Papa ... 46
12 Great Depression Begins ... 51
13 More years *of* Adapting ... 59
14 Turmoil Everywhere ... 66
15 Growing Up *in* DC ... 71
16 Old Friends, New friends ... 76
17 High School ... 87
18 Clouds *of* War ... 94
19 Civie *to* G.I. ... 109
20 In Position ... 121
21 Kassel Changes Everything ... 128
22 My Mission ... 134

23 G.I. *to* Civie ... 147
24 New Life ... 161
25 Los Alamos ... 169
26 What Became *of* Us? ... 174
　　Afterword ... 179
　　A Memorial ... 181
　　Photo Gallery ... 183

The Backstory

It was midnight of the year 2000, and sounds of celebration erupted from nearby homes signaling that we had all lived through the year, the decade, even the century.

My husband Rudy and I fed three calendars to the flames that night: one recorded our medical appointments, nearly every square filled, Sundays mercifully blank; another tracked my job schedule, which in truth was nothing but unmet commitments; and the third commemorated the rare social engagement along with visits from a worried family. As 1999 died, each calendar became ash in the stone fireplace.

Rudy and I ever after referred to 1999 as The Year That Was.

In January, we each got the phone call from a doctor telling us "the news was not good." From then on, we traded and re-traded caregiver roles for patient roles, hospital chairs for hospital beds. Rudy had considered himself the sturdier one in our pair, but the fireplace flames knew better: his triple bypass surgery "with complications" trumped my cancer. In 1999 we came to believe in Mortality and found that she had lessons to teach. Tasks put off for years, decades, must now be done. Included in this list were our wills.

It also included Rudy's book.

He had long flirted with the idea of writing a memoir, but this was the first time I had heard him speak seriously about it. With both time on his hands and an increasing sense of urgency, he declared, "I'm going to do this book. I'm going to write my story and keep you company."

And just like that, my dream of being captive to daytime television vanished. We agreed that my attention span during chemo—about five minutes on a good day—was just long enough to qualify me as editor for his book.

Finally ready to write his life story, one his family and friends had for years begged him to record, Rudy wrote quite unceasingly, easily capturing the perspectives and voices of himself as toddler, adolescent, and young man, as each took his turn living with Papa.

By this time, I had been married to Rudy for twenty years. I knew many stories of the German-born child raised in America's capital, carrying the label Enemy Alien even as he entered the US military. What I did not yet know was the depth of conflicting emotions that defined his relationship with his father: respect accompanied by fear, anger by love, pride by shame. Life with Papa was never simple or easy.

You may have met the adventurous adult Rudy in my account of our travels, *Rudy's Rules for Travel: Life Lessons from Around the Globe*. Told in his words, with my editorial input, this is the backstory—the story of how after a tumultuous upbringing, he came to live life one day at a time.

one

The Lucky Guys

US Army Eighth Air Force Base, World War II
Tibenham Village, Norwich, England

September, 1944

Lucky guys. My B-24 crew was ordered to stand down that night, while their crew—the lucky ones—were cleared for the bombing mission over Kassel, Germany. I thought it was all a matter of numbers: when you had flown your thirty-five missions, you got a pass back to the States. Those guys would be home before us, before Christmas if their luck continued—if their luck got them missions every day or night.

But before long I learned there are two kinds of luck: one that sends you into the sky and one that keeps you out. And there are also two kinds of time: the kind on the clock and the borrowed kind. I was starting to live on the borrowed version.

We were already suited up in flight gear when our Commanding Officer told us we didn't qualify for that night's strategic mission. "You're too new here," he announced. "You need more practice for night flying, especially for those blackouts on the ground. Report to the training area." Looking straight at us, his voice was firmer: "Now."

I felt my blood pressure rise as my best friend, our navigator Jeffrey, moved close to me. He instinctively stayed near my right elbow, ready to hold me back if my anger pushed me toward the C.O. Adding insult, the crewmen who were to take our place in formation that night had been chosen from our own barracks. I wanted to know just how many more trainings these guys had had, but Jeffrey was back on alert, pulling me to the corner of the room behind a tall locker, my anger out of sight of the officer.

We finished our spiritless training flights that night, with neither our hearts nor our minds in the exercises. I for one couldn't stop thinking of those lucky guys. *I must be more homesick than I thought. But Christ, who would be homesick for my home?*

From my bunk that night, I heard soft drones of planes circling overhead, joining other fleets from nearby bases, moving into formation for their flight across the English Channel to Germany. The rhythmic humming was strangely comforting, but the night itself was exceptionally icy. Our barracks had been hastily built from metal sheets and used lumber when the American base was set up, giving scant protection from the bitter winds of Southern England. I knew, though, that the crews overhead worked in far more frigid conditions, flying in the open-structure planes up to 25,000 feet, encountering temperatures as low as -50 degrees. Not even an electric suit could totally protect a flyer. As night went on,

Father and Son

I had to admit to myself that I so enjoyed the warmth of my thick down comforter that I no longer envied the men overhead in the dark cold.

Eventually it would be time for reconciliation, for giving our barracks mates the traditional welcome back. Those guys had stolen our place on the mission roster and they'd be going home before we were, but all would be forgiven. The men, after all, shared in our late-night poker games and our stories, mostly about the beautiful blondes we had all left behind at home.

Thirty-nine planes and over 300 men had taken off that night from our base, due back at 1:40 that afternoon. After lunch, Jeffrey and I borrowed bikes from the mess hall and rode out to the runway's end, ready to greet the first planes as they came in. We wanted to feel their wingspreads over our heads, to wave and cheer. I loved the welcoming ritual and could hardly wait until my own crew and plane came back some day to the cheers.

Usually, there was a triumphant howl of engines as planes passed low. But we could only see planes high overhead, traveling back to their own base, one well beyond ours. As intently as we looked, we could see no sign of the 39 bomber planes that carried the men who left us the night before. Rows of officers lined the control tower, scanning the sky through binoculars and shaking their heads, apparently seeing nothing either.

Jeffrey and I stood for what seemed like hours, scanning the sky repeatedly. It was not the first time I'd felt the conflicting emotions of shock, sorrow, grief, relief, and guilt. Eventually, our Commanding Officer climbed down from the control tower and walked slowly to us, staring at the ground between footsteps, conveying that he had a message he did not want to deliver. When he spoke, he looked straight at us, his soft tone unfamiliar:

"You can't stand here forever, sons. You can't just keep waiting."

Sons? He doesn't know, but I have had a lot of practice in waiting.

two

Waiting

Hamburg, Germany

1923

I was two years old when Mother died and Papa went back to sea. Much later, he tried to explain it all to me—why he'd sold his tavern on the Hamburg wharf, why he'd left to work on a big ship again, how he'd found a loving caregiver for me in Hamburg, and how he and I would someday go to America. I just needed to wait.

In the Hamburg, Germany depot, the steamer line posted dates the big ships were due to arrive, but my foster mother, Frau Kowenhagen, didn't put much stock in those notices. She thought it best to go to the wharf and look for Papa every day the sun shone. Dressed in the navy sailor uniform she made for me, I practiced my walking and waving as each boat came into the channel and sailed toward us. The crews blew loud whistles while passengers on deck waved to me and to my guard dog, Benno, a Doberman pinscher.

One day, after what must have been many months of waiting and greeting ships, a massive ocean liner approached the dock and we could see its name—the *SS George Washington*. "Rudy, Rudy, here comes your Papa," the Frau said. "He's here now." She had often talked to me about Papa, enough for me to understand this was someone I should be happy to see.

But instead of joy or even relief at finally meeting this Papa, I felt terror as a heavy, tall seaman came down the gangplank of the towering ocean liner, a weathered sea bag slung over his shoulder, black whiskers and a beard covering nearly his entire face. *Surely this could not be Papa.* But then the big man called my name and walked to me, fetching me from behind the Frau where I clung to her apron. "It's your Papa," she whispered, gently untangling my fingers and moving me toward the man.

Even as a young child, I was learning that emotions can be complicated. Frau and her teenaged daughter Herta were the only family I knew. But when this huge figure scooped me up in his arms, his nearness and warmth were new and exciting for me, and I was no longer afraid of him. When he hugged me and pressed his face against mine—whiskers and all—I began to feel that this Papa really was something nice in my life.

I recall one or two other times when Papa came from the sea, finding me at our wharf where I was waiting with the Frau. Each short visit was marked by some kind of fun or magic: going to parades, to the zoo, to dinner. I was amazed at his secret powers. Just by raising one arm he could bring a bright red taxi whooshing to the curb to take us somewhere.

Father and Son

But then, Papa also had the ability to disappear. After the short visits, he would climb the long stairway to the top deck of the massive ship, and I would go back to my waiting.

three

Papa: A First Look

My father, Carl Christian Jensen, was as complex as the feelings I had toward him. He could at once be gruff and loving, or determined and aimless. His six foot, three-hundred-pound figure could either shelter or intimidate me. I respected him and feared him at the same time.

Papa was born in Denmark in the year 1900, the ninth child of a respected Danish sea captain. Yet it would be his identification with Germany that would define much of his life. It would define much of my own life too. Papa so admired that nation and its culture that he wanted nothing more than to have a son born a German citizen. That took a little doing since I was conceived in America of a Hungarian woman and a Danish man, but Papa was not one to abandon his dreams.

I never knew my Grandfather Simon but his heritage was firmly ingrained in his son, my Papa, who had had inherited his father's love of the ocean and his affection for the German culture. My grandfather skippered a small freighter that navigated hard-to-reach ports in Norway and Denmark. Late in his career, grandfather Simon accepted a prestigious job as captain of a large world-trade freighter, and he happily moved his large family to a home near the wharf in the bustling city of Hamburg. For over three generations that wharf played a central role in the life of my family. However, the dream was not to last: grandfather Simon died shortly after assuming his new job.

My Papa was not the youngest child for long. His mother went on to remarry and give birth to five more babies. Undoubtedly the family home grew crowded.

At fourteen, my father swung a knapsack over his shoulder and followed the siren call of the sea, just as his father had done at nearly the same age. When so often I am drawn to the ocean, to both its beauty and its peril, it may well be the pull of two generations.

Before I was born, Papa worked at least a decade on a variety of vessels, first as a cabin boy, then as a deck steward and waiter on ocean-crossing liners that brought large numbers of German immigrants from Hamburg to New York City. He never desired to be ship's captain as his father had been. "Too much responsibility," he said. He preferred equal relationships with his mates, the comradeship of a crew, the ability to "hoist a few" as the ship sailed on in the night.

Though he physically lived on land almost all the years I knew him, Papa never truly left the sea. He held fast to the need to be "his own man," to be independent like the journeyer. And he never lost his desire to learn. As an adult, I have often wondered how it was that, with an eighth-grade education, Papa could recite long texts of German poetry, sing lyrics with the Metropolitan Opera on the radio, and memorize lengthy political tracts to share with friends. In another age and time, given schooling and control over the worst of his habits, Papa might have been a professor or a politician. Instead, he focused his aspiration on a new goal: immigrating to America. The combination of his personal experience in then-prosperous America and hearing the aspirations of his passengers fostered his desire to make a home in the new land.

As the First World War began in 1914, Papa's work on the liners faded: in wartime the ocean was less safe and attracted fewer passengers for crossings. Taking an elongated shore leave, he apprenticed in several luxurious hotel restaurants in New York City and Washington, DC. I have always wondered whether, despite his pronounced loyalty to Germany, he was avoiding that country's draft during World War I.

Once the war ended, he returned to sea, working aboard one of the finest ships in Germany's Hamburg-American line, regularly sailing between Hamburg and New York. As a waiter and deck steward, Papa had unlimited opportunity to meet "the lovely ladies," as he called them. But none could compare with the beautiful and vivacious Hungarian woman he discovered in New York City.

four

My First Mother

New York City
Washington, DC

1920

Although Papa did not earn the wages of a bon vivant, he had a gourmet's taste. When on ship layovers in New York City, he frequented a Hungarian restaurant on Thirty-Ninth Street, captivated by the old-world ambiance, fine paprika-laced foods, and soft strains of the violins. One night, most captivating of all, was the woman seated at the window table.

Francisca was indeed beautiful and vivacious, but she was also married. New York did not look kindly upon divorce, and neither did the elderly husband with whom she was seated. She and Henry Hirsch had been married twelve years. Like many other wealthy immigrants to America at the time, Henry had returned to his home village in Hungary to seek a young bride, giving her family a handsome monetary reward for arranging the marriage. Arranged marriages were not intended to end in divorce, but Papa was not one to give up a quest.

Love at first sight persisted for months and was strong enough to conquer both Francisca's husband and strict state law: in New York City, an incident of adultery was among reasons that could legally qualify a couple to file for divorce. The adultery needed to be verified by a competent, reputable witness who could testify under oath that he or she saw the married individual enter a hotel with someone other than his/her spouse and spend most of the day or night in the company of that person. It was common practice to employ a private investigator to act as witness, and that is what my father did. I never quite understood what the surveillance of Francisca entailed; Papa, in telling me this story, left out details that would have intrigued me as a teenager and still do today.

Was the investigator watching the hotel entrance from across the street, huge binoculars in hand and pressed up against the window glass?

Or was he simply in the hotel lounge, drink in hand, timing their rendezvous and waiting for them to emerge?

Or, just possibly, did he have to get closer to the event?

Her divorce final, the newly married couple moved from New York City to Washington, DC., where they settled down in a small but comfortable upstairs apartment. (Note here that this is not the last we will hear of Henry Hirsch.) My mother, apparently an industrious woman, soon opened a corset shop on the ground floor. Papa, exchanging love of the sea for love of Francisca, turned in his seaman's identification papers and secured a position as a waiter in the opulent Willard Hotel restaurant, which catered to senators and federal officials, most notably J. Edgar Hoover and his FBI officers. In time, Hoover noted Papa's European manners and began to request "Carl's table" for his luncheon meetings. A long-term friendship with Papa began, one that would intertwine the two in years ahead.

Francisca's business was becoming successful. Papa's job was prestigious and paid well. The apartment suited them. But Papa was Papa, and as Francisca grew more comfortable, he grew more restless.

five

My First Voyage

1920

Anyone who knew Papa guessed that he would soon become disenchanted with life as a worker in Washington, DC. Taking direction from employers was not one of his talents, even if that direction was part of a well-paying job in the well-to-do Willard Hotel. The Willard was so alive with politics and politicians in that era that its lobby inspired the word "lobbyists."

While most men in those times would likely crave Papa's job, as well as the love and security of his new marriage, Papa experienced his life as constrained. A seaman at heart since his fourteenth birthday when he joined the hard-drinking, risk-taking crewmen's society onboard the Hamburg America ships, not even the beauty of his new wife could ease the wanderlust.

One winter morning in 1920, Francisca set the breakfast table with fine white china and an arrangement of camellias, unable to wait until the meal was ready to share her news: she was pregnant. Papa was ecstatic. A major change was about to occur in their lives, and Papa relished change. But one significant shift was not enough.

In the early years of the twentieth century, it was not uncommon for the man of the household to make all decisions for the family, even life-changing ones. In this case, Father decided to open his own business, where he could be his own boss and make all the rules—and he would do it in Hamburg. He bought a tavern in a seaport he knew well, serving food and drink (mostly drink) to all his old friends. In later years, I learned that opening the saloon was Papa's secondary motive for moving to Germany, the first being his insistence that his first child be born a German citizen.

As many times as I think about this, I cannot understand Papa's nationalistic fervor. The move was not at all consistent with his apparent lack of patriotism for Germany during World War I, nor even more strangely, with his true heritage as a Dane. But then, Papa was not known for consistency.

There were multiple elements that argued against this plan. My mother's homeland was Hungary; she had never stepped foot in Germany. She ran a successful business in the United States capitol. She was pregnant with me. Papa's job paid well. I imagine that she and Papa had more than a few conversations about his dream. Yet, eventually it took hold, and the decision would greatly alter their lives—and my own.

And so, nearly six months pregnant, Francisca closed her thriving corset business, sold the apartment furnishings, and carefully packed the most precious of her china and linens. As a wanderer, always ready to move on to the next adventure, her husband had virtually nothing to pack or sell. He fit all his worldly possessions into his sailor's knapsack and threw them over his shoulder.

During the stormy, mid-winter crossing of the North Atlantic from New York to Hamburg, my mother suffered mightily from *mal de mer*. Combined with her pregnancy, I assume the trip was tortuous for her. I do believe my father loved her, but I have no difficulty also believing the accounts of his friends at the time. They say he had chosen the ship because it was manned by old acquaintances from his earlier days as a crewman. After their work shifts, Papa joined his friends below deck for parties, just like the good old days.

Just as was true of the lives of my grandfather and father, the North Atlantic Ocean was a major character in my life story. Beginning with this voyage, sheltered in the body of my mother, I made a series of Atlantic crossings. I would travel that turbulent ocean again in 1925 as a toddler under highly unusual circumstances, then in the mid-1940s twice more, first sailing to war with other young, healthy airmen, then returning home with my severely wounded mates from German P.O.W. camps and hospitals.

Soon after we arrived at the bustling Hamburg seaport, Papa spotted what he saw as a perfect opportunity. The combination business and home lay one block from the wharf that had been so prominent in the life of his father, the one that had seen young Papa leave on his first worldwide journey.

Father and Son

The Rappabahn was a lively street that ran parallel to the docks, one block from the harbor, prime real estate for brothels and saloons. It had worldwide notoriety among thirsty, lonely sailors and merchant seamen. At sea for months, the men had been deprived of intimacy and companionship, and the bargain was clear: the Rappabahn would make it all up to them as the beneficiary of their wages from their long months of hard work at sea.

The property Papa found seemed to meet everyone's needs—a spacious upstairs apartment in which to raise a baby, space for a small corseting business, and a large downstairs restaurant with a tavern. As you might suspect, the restaurant with tavern functioned more like a saloon with occasional sandwich orders, and it did not take long before Papa was known as the most genial bartender in all the Rappabahn. Short of money? Have sea stories to share? Papa could run a long tab for you and swap tales through the night. And when his old shipmates came into port, the tabs and stories grew even longer.

Not many people have the distinction of being born above a saloon. I came into this world on May 17, 1921—just three months after our trip across the sea from America—in our upstairs apartment on an exceptionally bright sunny day. Mother later wrote to her relatives, saying she had had a comparatively easy delivery, assisted by a kindly doctor, one of Papa's frequent customers.

My birth was a local occasion: as first born of the affable bartender and his lovely wife, I hear I did not lack for attention in this, shall we say, seedy part of Germany. But the Rappebahn was hardly a place for a young family, and Papa worried for our safety. Just after I turned one, Papa found a purebred German Doberman pinscher who guarded us day and night. His name was Benno, loaned to my family by a sailor who never returned for him. I vaguely remember the dog, but the pictures of him with me clarify why no one would come near us, let alone harm us. Muzzled and tightly leashed, he walked stiffly beside my perambulator. It took a lot of courage to make friends with Benno and few people made the grade. All that sternness was reserved, though, for his professional role on public streets. At home, my father told me later, he was my gentle, curled-up-on-the-thick-rug companion. My favorite sleeping position, Papa remembered, was stretched atop Benno, my head tucked between his long, pointed ears.

Just before my second birthday, I lost my guard and companion. Papa had taken Benno to visit an old friend who had just arrived on a large freighter. Mother and I came walking along the wharf sometime later. When Benno spotted the two of us, he used his taut muscles to slip his leash, break away from father, and race toward Mother and me. Attempting to leap across an open hatch, he fell short of its far edge and plunged through the opening, falling three decks down to his instant death. All of us sobbed and mourned his loss for months.

It wasn't long before our grieving was eclipsed by another sudden death, a tragic loss that Papa was never to recover from, one that would leave me confused and alone.

Six

Loss

Hamburg, Germany

Spring, 1923

I have never been able to construct a clear memory of my mother, Francisca. I have a photograph of her, but it is not the same as having a picture of her in my mind, not the same as being able to conjure up images of our two years together. She brought me into this world; surely, she must have been central in my young life. But still as I write this now, over seventy years after her death, I find myself deeply regretting my loss of her memory.

I am told that we had a fine celebration of my second birthday. Two tall candles sat atop a chocolate cake big enough to share with the tavern customers, and I met my new teddy bear, one nearly as large as myself. He could not replace my dog Benno, but he was nonetheless a sweet companion.

Just a few weeks later, my mother suddenly became seriously ill, suffering from gall bladder disease. In modern times, conditions like gall bladder attacks are commonly experienced and handled by doctors with ease, but they were still unconquerable in the early twentieth century. In only a short time, the disease claimed her life. I was too immature to understand what had happened, to recognize the permanence of death. Maybe that is one way in which nature protects its very young, shielding them from such harsh reality.

Papa was devastated. The dreams he had fashioned for their lives dissolved the night she passed away. In their young marriage, every aspect of their lives was entwined. Both his love for her and his need for her had been intense, and I suspect she had provided the stability he so lacked in her absence.

After my mother was gone, the tavern no longer held allure for Papa. He could not join in the raucous parties of the sailors, and upstairs, the apartment was painfully too large. With no need for the downstairs business space, he quickly sold it all and headed back to what he knew: the sea.

Just as I have no memory of my mother and her death, I have no recollection of the days Papa left from the Hamburg dock, setting sail on the trans-Atlantic liner. He would be gone up to ten months or a year at a time. What I do recall from that period is the warm embrace of Frau Kowenhagen.

Though he left abruptly, Papa arranged well for my care. The Frau had lost her husband at sea several years earlier and she needed extra income. She seemed happy to have the chance to help my grieving family, and her teenage daughter, Herta, became my needed sibling. I lived only two years with these loving people, but it always surprises me how vivid the memories of those years were.

For one example, I recall happily running through my new neighborhood, rolling my bright red-and-blue wooden hoop, when I suddenly stumbled on a raised cobblestone, gashing my left knee on its sharp corner. I still bear a deep one-inch scar on that knee, one that perhaps symbolizes others that lay beneath the surface. What I remember most, though, is the soft, comforting clucks my kind caretaker made as she and Herta ministered to my wound. Once recovered, I became fond of flying through the streets of Hamburg sitting snuggly in the sidecar of my Uncle Willie's motorcycle. Uncle Willie was my father's younger stepbrother, whose visits provoked both horror and chagrin in Frau Kowenhagen.

Herta was my more constant companion, with whom I practiced my cobblestone walking in the streets of Old Hamburg. We spent time at the city zoo, which I loved, but my favorite excursion was to the sandy beaches of Blanke Nase, a popular recreation area near the mouth of the Elbe River where it entered the North Sea. I remember Herta carrying my shovel and bucket so that I might build a sandcastle alongside those of other toddlers, all of us watching the freighters entering and leaving the port of Hamburg just yards ahead of us. My friends and I screamed in delight both at the mighty, earth-shaking blasts from the huge ships' steam horns and at the sharp whistles of small tugboats giving directions to the liners.

The pleasure I got from our days at the beach was second only to the excitement of preschool, a privilege given to three-year-olds of the city. My favorite game was "Ring Around the Rosie." I loved it best when my pals and I all fell down, giggling and tumbling over each other. I have since lost the black-and-white photo, but I recall seeing it as I grew up: my little classmates and I holding hands and looking into the camera with what appears to be terror, or at least apprehension. This is likely because photographers were not common then, and children were understandably wary of the man who disappeared under a black cloth before a bright light seemed to explode from his hand.

One day, my faith in my foster sister Herta was put to the test. Two people in my life had already disappeared, and one fall afternoon, as it grew dark, I thought she had left me too. This is one of those memories I would just as soon not retain: a densely wooded city park was one of our favorite playgrounds until I failed to learn all the rules of Hide and Go Seek. I was proud of a new skill—running fast and hiding behind big trees. The part I did not understand was that you should stay within finding distance of your guardian, especially if the sky is darkening and the air is beginning to whistle through the trees. I searched and searched for Herta, running in circles, but she was nowhere. Suddenly, I realized I was alone among those looming somber trees. When a three-year-old is faced with a dilemma like this, there is only one thing to do: cry. And I did—long and loud—until suddenly there was Herta. She gave me a huge hug and off we went to home.

I still have photos of myself from this period, and although my memories of these two years are generally happy, the pictures tell a different story. The photographs portray a sad little boy apparently confused, clinging to his teddy bear, staring ahead with expressionless eyes. I do not know which is more accurate, the memories or the photos, or if perhaps life was simply hard to figure out in those years.

seven

Four-Year-Old Sailor

Hamburg, Germany to New York City

1925

During the two years I lived with the Frau and her daughter, I had two or three visits from Papa. I don't recall missing him when he was gone, but I do recall having fun when we were together. The circus, city parks, walks on the dock beside the towering man—I liked it all. And each time he left he'd make me happy with his promise: "Someday you and I will go to America. We'll live there, maybe in one of those big houses. Just you wait."

I was puzzled. I had no idea what this "America" was. What I did know, though, was that I wanted to go where Papa went.

Two years went by and the Frau took me often to the dock to see if Papa's ship might have returned early. It was a chance to practice my waving and walking as the other big liners came into port. Passengers lined the decks and waved back but, usually, no

Papa. The Frau and Herta reassured me every time, saying, "Just you wait, Rudy."

At last, the Frau received word that I was to sail to America on the next ship, the *SS George Washington*. Papa wrote that he was arranging passage for me. Alone. He needed to stay in America and would await me there. Booking a lone four-year-old for a twelve- to fourteen-day sea voyage would be unheard of today; presumably, it was unusual even in 1925. But Papa's connections to the seafaring world ran deep. He located some of his old sailor friends, those he considered most trustworthy, to watch over me on the liner. To this day I do not know if I was a stowaway or an honored guest, or perhaps something in between.

The Frau sewed a new navy-colored sailor suit for me, and stuffed a duffel bag with necessities for the journey to New York. My long blonde curls stuck out from under my captain's hat and my new shoes gleamed. They were Mary Janes, a style only girls wear now (and maybe then too). During his last visit, Papa had taught me how to salute the ship's officers, and the Frau helped me practice my new skill.

As an adult, I can well imagine the distress my caregiver and her daughter felt as they left the little sailor on the deck of the massive liner. As an adult, I have also wondered if some of Frau's distress came from the newly broken connection between her and my father. I'll never know if she was in love with him, but many women were.

I have very little memory of the journey. I don't recall even meeting Papa's "most trustworthy sailor friends," the ones who had pledged to watch over me. I do recall that I had my own snug bunk, sharing a first-class cabin and my meals with two friendly elderly ladies who must have adopted me for the journey, making sure all my needs were met.

The North Atlantic crossing was known for its storms, felt particularly on the 1920s liners that lacked stabilizers. Strangely, I don't remember turbulent seas, but I do remember one particular day onboard when it was exceptionally bright and windy on deck. The captain gave me and the children I played with handfuls of bright-colored inflated balloons. My new little companions and I released the balloons over the stern of the ship and watched with great delight as they sailed up and away across a brilliant blue sea. Mine were red, and I could see them floating for a long time.

Although my recall of the voyage itself is dim, I have a distinct and happy picture in my mind of finding Papa. As our big liner slowed and pulled into one of the docks in the New York harbor, I heard a boisterous call —"Rudy, Rudy, here I am"—and I spotted him waving to me from far below the rail where I stood. He kept calling until he heard my answering cry: "Papa, Papa! Here I am!"

I must have been tired from the voyage, because the next thing I remember is waking in a fancy room, cozily snuggled up to the massive, warm body of Papa. I didn't realize it then, but I later learned that we had spent my first night in America in the luxurious Waldorf Astoria Hotel in midtown Manhattan. This stay must have made a deep impression on me because I can tell you every detail of that room, right down to the soft pink lights that flowed from the bedside lamps, and the breakfast a waiter served to us right in our bed. I had soft-boiled eggs with raisin bread toast and Papa read his newspaper right next to me. When he was finished, he told me we would leave in a few hours for Washington, a big city in America, and ride on a very large train. Best of all, he said, when we got to that city, I would meet my new Mutti. ("Mutti" is a German endearment, much as "Mommy" is in English.) We would travel today and we would find her, this Mutti.

When we arrived, Papa and I knocked on a heavy door in a modest apartment house in Washington, DC. A petite brunette, a young German woman Papa called Anna, welcomed us with a warm smile. She bent down right away to look at me and tell me she would like to be my Mutti. I believe I understood immediately that she was someone very, very special.

Anna led me into a room at the back of the apartment, a room she had clearly prepared for a four-year-old boy. It was bright, sunny, and all mine. I had never had a room to myself and it was thrilling. The new wallpaper, hung just for me, had colorful circus figures: clowns and animals cavorting around the wall and bright tents forming a happy background.

A freshly painted white desk and chair stood in the corner. "You'll go to American school, Rudy, and you'll want to study," she said. I tried on the chair for size and my feet dangled far above the floor.

Mutti and Papa were quick to assure me that I would be growing fast, now that we were all together. And another surprise—I had a roommate. I would be sharing all this splendor with a big gray tomcat of dubious heritage whose name was

Barrie. The now formidable cat had grown from the tiny kitten given to my father by another employee, the cigarette girl at the Williard Hotel. Life was quite complete.

eight

A New Mother

Washington, DC

1924

I was right. Mutti was special. My luck was turning. Through the years of our lives together it was she who would be my constant loving guide and mentor, healer of bruises and scratches, the steady presence always there for me. With each childhood day, I grew closer to her.

As an adult, I think often of the many sacrifices she made in her attempt to give me a stable and loving home. Surely the life she led in her new country was quite different from the one she had imagined when she left Germany to travel those stormy seas. She also most certainly discovered that there is more than one kind of storm.

Like Papa, my new mother came from a large family. The Webers raised ten children in southern Bavaria's Friedrichshaven, a picture-perfect town on Lake Constance where her father was a railroad supervisor. They would ordinarily have been considered a middle-class family, but World War I ravaged their lives.

Soon after hostilities were declared in 1914, Mutti's two eldest brothers, Max and Franz, both in their early twenties, were drafted into the German army. Only ten months later, both were killed in the trenches somewhere in France. At home the family repeatedly suffered food shortages, using potatoes as their main nutrition and making "coffee" from dried-up and ground turnips. Sugar was virtually unknown. Because coal for heating was in such short supply, like other German families they began burning furniture, fencing, or anything combustible to keep warm. The youngest children were sent each day to scavenge along miles of railroad tracks, searching for lumps of coal that might have fallen from passing trains.

Mutti and her sisters left school after the required eighth grade, seeking jobs at the nearby Zeppelin factory to help support the family. Because the factory was heavily engaged in turning out the rigid balloon-shaped airships for the German military, sixteen-year-old Anna worked ten- or twelve-hour days. She told me later that the hardest part of the workday was walking the few blocks to and from the factory. Because it was impossible to replace aged shoes, she and her sisters had to stuff theirs with old newspapers, an almost reasonable solution until the snows came.

The Webers looked forward to the day World War I would end and normalcy would return. Instead, defeated Germany plunged for decades into economic and political chaos, distress that seemed endless. The country's unemployment rate and already high inflation ran rampant. The victorious Allies' repatriation demands created additional layers of national debt. Years of hunger and discontent eventually formed the fertile soil in which a man like Adolf Hitler and a political party like the Nazis were able to gain control of the rudderless ship of state.

In the midst of the turmoil, Anna saw a flyer advertising an opportunity to begin a new life in America. Despite being one of the nations that had defeated Germany, it welcomed Europeans to, as the flyer said, "the land of opportunity and equality." American families would pay the second-class one-way fare for immigrants willing to work one year as indentured servants in their homes. After the year, they would be free to find other employment in the United States. Anyone not fulfilling the year satisfactorily would repay the employer/sponsor for their passage. It was deemed a risky situation, since the employer was sole judge of what "satisfactory" meant. But if one was to seek a new life, freed of old traditions, there were risks to be taken.

As an intelligent and responsible worker, Anna had consistently received promotions at the Zeppelin factory. She signed up for the indenture program confident she would fulfill the expectations, though she did not know when or if she would ever see her home and family again.

While I waited for Papa in Hamburg in the spring of 1924, he was employed as the deck steward for second-class passengers on the Hamburg American liner, carrying immigrants to New York City. Papa was responsible for the well-being of his passengers: cabin assignments, dining room reservations, and, in bad weather, sympathy. The first day at sea, he discovered petite Anna clinging to the rail as the ship lurched into the turbulent North Atlantic. Decks were awash with high waves breaking over the plunging prow of the ship as it forced its way westward into the teeth of the storm. The young woman was questioning her decision to leave home, but in the midst of the crashing waves, there was no backing down now.

As the worst of this first storm abated, most of the passengers' complexions reflected varied shades of green. Father later told me that even in the midst of so many suffering fellow travelers, Anna seemed more pathetic than most in her discomfort. He insisted that was why he gave her special attention, bringing her cup after cup of medicinal teas. His kindness to Anna led to further conversations. Father, as fluent in German as he was in Danish, learned that she was indentured as a nanny and housekeeper to a family in a suburb of Trenton, New Jersey.

By the time the liner docked in the New York harbor, my father and this young lady were fast friends. They continued to see each other through the year of her servitude, sandwiching in visits between father's trips across the Atlantic and her days off work. Time passed slowly for them, but eventually her indentured year was complete. They were married in a New York City civil ceremony well attended by my father's cronies from the ship and by Anna's employer and his large family.

Papa and Anna moved to Washington, DC, rented a small apartment, and began the process of sending for me. Father once again turned in his sailor's identification badge and re-established himself as a waiter at the Williard Hotel, while Anna set about making the apartment a cheerful, spotlessly clean home for her new family.

The turbulent North Atlantic Sea had starred again in my life, this time bringing me a loving new mother. In the joy of their early days, however, there was no way the couple could have foreseen that the suffering of the Weber family, and the agony of Germany after World War I, would reach down into my life as a young man.

nine

Fitting In

Washington, DC

1926

It took me reaching adulthood to realize how complex my family heritage was. Papa was 100 percent Danish but a German loyalist who had moved heaven and earth (and a pregnant wife) to have his son born a German citizen, but had not himself served in Germany's War. Mutti was a southern German whose family had been deeply scarred by World War I. Though half Danish and half Hungarian, I was nonetheless a German citizen, being raised as a German child in America's capital city. The three of us believed that sailing to America had brought us to a better life, a far better life, in fact. Not one of us likely thought of how our family would forever be influenced by our diverse loyalties.

In the first months of my life in Washington DC, I lived in what you might call a German bubble. Our closest neighbors in the apartment house were German; our little grocery store was managed by a family from Mutti's region; father's shipmate friends were all from Hamburg. Our only news came from the weekly paper Papa borrowed from German customers at the hotel and from the steady stream of letters from Friedrichshaven. When Mutti and I took our walks, we were greeted with *"Guten Morgen"* rather than "Good Morning."

But my comfortable, sheltered life was about to change.

When I turned five, it was time I met kindergarten. Though "kindergarten" itself is a German word, that did not help at all. The first lesson I got was in being different. I had not been exposed to English, and I was suddenly surrounded by children and adults who talked fast in some kind of gibberish I could not begin to understand. They seemed to want me to do things, but I had no idea what those things were. I still remember the kind teacher and some of the children who tried so hard to help me. Nonetheless, I spent much of every school day crying bitter tears in this strange land.

Perhaps no one wanted to tell Mutti that my difference was not just in language. She had taken great pains to dress me for school, searching in the fabric shop for the perfect material and sewing two fine outfits. These were the days when boys and girls lined up outside their classrooms after recess or lunchtime—and I was constantly being placed in the girls' line. Photographs of me during this time period show why: I am dressed in Lord Fauntleroy short pants, a blouse-like buttoned top, embroidered suspenders, and knee socks. My curly golden locks had never been cut: they cascaded below my shoulders and over my wide blue eyes.

The days at school dragged on, with me struggling to understand the language and my classmates struggling to understand me. One night at home, my parents had a long discussion. I listened in and heard them decide two things must happen if I was to succeed in American schools. First, the long blonde curls had to go, since even in the neighborhood I was being mistaken for a little girl. Second, I must learn the language of America.

The next day, poor Mutti sat in the corner of the barber shop, crying all the way through the ordeal. When it was over, she picked up a particularly well-curled swatch of yellow hair from the floor, placed it in an envelope she had brought with her, and labeled it in German, "Little Rudy's Locks, 1925." That envelope has survived all these years. Gradually, my wardrobe was also transformed: Mutti began sewing me long pants and button-down shirts, and she found a warm coat for my Washington winter.

Selflessly, my parents were determined to use English as their daily language in our home. Papa had already gained fluency in his earlier years by visiting America, avidly reading English-language books, listening to radio commentary at every opportunity, and interacting with colleagues and hotel customers. But it was not an easy commitment for Mutti: she had no early exposure to the language and was struggling to learn even basic phrases. Luckily, Father was an excellent model for both mother and me. In later years, Mutti became quite competent in writing and speaking English, although she maintained a slight southern (I thought charming) German accent all her life.

By year's end, I must have made some progress in my kindergarten lessons because I was promoted to first grade. Miss Haberman was a kind and caring teacher, but I presented more challenges than she was prepared for. My language development simply wasn't at the level of my classmates, and I was retained for another semester. I don't recall any open discussion of this at home, but I do remember spending a good deal of time at the white desk in my room, with Barrie the Tomcat monitoring my homework.

Life at school gradually improved over the years, but I tended not to be a particularly good student. My strengths in art and reading seemed always counterbalanced by weaknesses in arithmetic and—yes—conduct. Apparently, my language skills developed *too* well. My report cards throughout my elementary years were tiresome in their complaints about my talking too much to myself and to others and not being cooperative with classroom rules. I still have the report card from Miss Allen in fifth grade who, writing with a heavy hand and a thick-nibbed black pen, blazed large letters across one whole side of my card: "STOP TALKING TO SELF!" Though I never got into serious trouble, I was a child whose behavior was just marginal enough to get under the teacher's skin.

Who would have guessed that one day I would lean across a big maple desk in my office and tell worried parents that there were advantages to their little boy repeating first grade. "Being a bit older than others in his class might give him a little extra edge," I'd say. "I could share a story with you if you have time."

ten

Prohibition and the Family

Washington, DC

1929

The little apartment could not absorb the forces that swirled around it—Prohibition, the Great Depression, and Papa's drinking and partying. As an adult I see that Papa's risk-taking was a bit like Barrie's: impulsive and ready to face oncoming danger with scarcely a thought for consequences.

At the time, I was too young to understand that Papa had never truly left the lifestyle of the seaman. Habits formed when he was a teenager had not faded, and the Prohibition era only intensified his reliance on alcohol and "good times." I spent many nights straining to listen to Mutti and Papa's heated arguments through my bedroom door, trying to imagine what a "speakeasy" was, and why they didn't like each other anymore. Their arguments would end when one of them whispered, "Shhh, you'll wake him." That was my cue to snuggle with Barrie under the European coverlet, both of us pretending to be fast asleep when Mutti opened the door to check on us.

Over time, laughter with Barrie became a sharp contrast to the harsh atmosphere I felt growing between my parents. I began to understand that things were not all right. What I could not have understood then was how the tension between Mutti and Papa was most likely influenced by major social conditions of the time; both Prohibition and the beginning of the Great Depression probably played major roles.

The Prohibition Era had been in effect for nine years, since midnight on January 16, 1920, when a federal law was enacted that alcohol could not be manufactured or consumed. This type of legislation by a government could easily have been the cause of a major revolution in some other countries of the world (I'm thinking France!), but instead it spawned a whole new industry in America. By its very structure, Prohibition seemed to open the door for many citizens to profit handsomely as they skirted the law. Increasingly, bold and dangerous groups of gangsters controlled illegal sales of alcoholic beverages, while at the same time greased the palms of police departments.

"Speakeasy" described any place that surreptitiously served illegal beverages (at inflated prices) to "selected" customers. Most often the sources of liquor supply for these illegal private bars were crime syndicates operated by gangster organizations. Speakeasies that served whisky or beer were busy twenty-four hours a day, seven days a week, and especially on holidays. Police and city governments were often unable or unwilling to control these lawless operations, and much of the time they shared in the illegal profits by ignoring the obvious transgressions of the crime mob. This corruption of elected officials and lawmen was often looked upon as merely "profit sharing," a way for public officials to participate in the fast life that many were now enjoying. In addition to illegal booze, flappers, the Charleston, and 'hot' jazz were the superficial hallmarks of this Roaring Twenties era.

Not ready to cast off the free lifestyle he had enjoyed on the ships, my father was a frequent customer of several of these illegal nightclubs. Besides her worry about our dwindling family finances, Mutti lived in fear that Papa would be in one of his favorite bars on a night it was raided and patrons jailed. I believe he loved Mutti and me dearly but, as he described it, he had that "urge to hoist a few with the boys" after work. Unfortunately, his work at the hotel restaurant usually lasted until midnight.

Restaurant guests—including many congressmen—frequently lingered into the early-morning hours, enjoying their Havana cigars and secret sips of brandy from silver hip flasks. In these late hours, their conversation was filled with heavy political talk and government deal-making, and Papa took it all in. His European roots made him particularly interesting, with his tales of Germany's innocence and America's neglect. In addition, he always had a secret political story to tell in his loud and engaging fashion, making him a welcome customer. At about two o'clock each morning, having been on duty for so many hours, Papa felt justified in treating himself just as the senators treated themselves. He further enjoyed sharing the generous tips of his guests—not with his family, but with waiters at the speakeasies—and it was not unusual for his tip to exceed the cost of the meal.

I was about eight years old when I realized the problem between my parents was continuing to grow. After a hard week with Papa routinely coming home around three in the morning, his and Mutti's voices grew louder in the night. Not even my playful cat's distractions could lessen the tension in our home. We had no money in the till for the smallest of bills, so even when Barrie and I put on little shows for Papa and Mutti, they would laugh for a while at his tricks and then both grow silent.

One winter night I was awakened to find my dear Mutti bending over me and sobbing. Although the bedroom was dark, a light shone from outside in the hall, and I could see that she had her hat on and her little fox fur around her neck. Between her heavy sobs, she whispered to me that she was going to have to leave me and that she was probably never going to see me again. I can still hear her voice and see her as clearly as I did that night many years ago. Frightened and sad, I reached up and clasped my arms about her neck, crying bitterly, "Mutti, please please don't leave me. I don't want you to go away." I pulled her down so that she lay next to me in my bed, and we both cried a long, long time. Finally, she put her arms around me. "I can't leave you, my dear Rudy," she said. "I will stay with you always, no matter what happens. Don't worry. You go back to sleep now."

That is how close I came to losing my dear Mutti.

Over all these years, that night is emblazoned in my memory. I can replay every word, see Mutti's tears, feel what was to have been her last hug. Mutti of all people knew how difficult it was always going to be to live with Papa, to accept his spending, his late-night lifestyle. As I became a teenager, I could feel in myself the exasperation and helplessness she must have felt that night, and so many nights before, as she tried to confront her sturdy, stubborn husband.

When I tell people this story, they assume my father had had an affair, leaving Mutti hurt and enraged. But I asked her once and she was adamant: my father had many faults, very many faults, she said, but unfaithfulness was not one of them. Neither was physical abuse. Papa could lose his temper, but when he did, he did not strike; he merely left the room noisily, remaining behind a closed door. Perhaps his seafaring life had taught him self-control. Certainly, his stature and skill with language spared him combat: when one is over six feet tall, weighs a muscular three hundred pounds, and can verbally level an opponent, fists are superfluous. As an adult I realize now that Mutti had no legal right to my custody. I was Papa's child, his German child. When Mutti bent over me to say goodbye that night, she truly believed she would likely never see me again.

This life of poverty and conflict surely was not the American dream Mutti had envisioned when she left Germany, sailing alone across the North Atlantic. She was one of those immigrants whom the ocean had betrayed. For a few weeks after that traumatic night, the early-morning arguments were somewhat quieter, and Barrie and I often got a whole night's sleep. Over time, the volume and pitch of disagreements increased, but she never again threatened to leave. Each morning, for fifteen years, my mother stirred oatmeal on the stove and poured me an extra glass of milk as Papa slept. I often question what would have happened to me, what kind of life I would have had, who would have given me much-needed course correction as a teenager, if she had left that night.

eleven

Another Look at Papa

Washington, DC

1929

My father had his faults, and they surfaced often in the life of our family—but he also had virtues and talents that enriched our lives and endeared him to us.

Although his parents could not afford to give their thirteen children an education beyond the state-sponsored eight years, Papa was knowledgeable in several cultural fields. The world itself must have been his teacher. His knapsack was filled with volumes of poetry, novels, history, and political texts. He not only read favorite poets—such as Goethe and Schiller—but he memorized favored works. Complex classic German poetry would not likely be taught in the lower years of public education, and I know he never set foot in a classroom beyond that level. I surmise my birth mother Francesca had shared a love of art and music with him, and that he followed through, using the time spent on long sea voyages to become a self-educated man.

After Papa left the sea, he continued every day to read in his three languages, supplementing classic literature with English and German magazines and newspapers he bought at the newsstand down the street. He was fascinated with the true detective stories that were popular in that day; like many of our neighbors, he waited eagerly for the next monthly installments. He also kept abreast of European news, insisting he knew as much about what was happening in those nations as the columnists did.

Papa was never one to keep his talents and insights to himself. He knew a lot about fine cuisine from working in the luxury hotels. He was a good chef and loved to entertain at dinners, filling the small apartment with German friends for a sauerbraten meal. They were appreciative as well as captive audiences. His entertainment included recitations of complex German poetry, after which guests applauded his "wondrous expression." Even I knew that his recitations got more wondrous with every drink.

Frequently Papa assigned me a short, almost conquerable poem to recite for our guests. Often, my memorization assignment resulted from a bit of a behavioral problem. I may have said or done something Papa deemed inappropriate—and Papa was the judge. To this day, out of nowhere a line from Schiller will appear in my mind. Surprisingly, it is never accompanied by any resentment of Papa.

After the poetry segment of our entertainment, Papa would often give his analysis of Germany's political and economic state. The evening typically concluded with Papa's singing or reciting the lyrics of a German, Italian, or French opera. Though Papa was

Danish, he favored the bombastic sounds of a Wagnerian piece.

Summer nights provided Papa with another audience for his recitals. This was long before air conditioning, and Washington DC was noted for its hot, sticky air that made it impossible for anyone to sleep in the cramped apartments, almost all of which lacked cross-ventilation. On the worst nights, we and our neighbors soaked bedsheets in our bathtubs, squeezed out excess water, and wrapped them tightly around our bodies. We then had two choices: sleep half-sitting on our small fire escape, or walk down the street garbed in sheets to lie in the grassy neighborhood park. No, we did not fear falling asleep surrounded by mostly strangers; besides having a level of trust in others that we don't enjoy in modern times, we all assumed that the DC air rendered our fellow sleepers as enervated and motionless as we were. Throughout the neighborhood, the grocer pushed his cart down the sidewalks, calling out rhythmically, "Ice cold watermelon, cold to the rind." Every so often we each bought the treat for three cents. From our apartment, Papa's poetry and music reached the fire escape sleepers, but did not drift as far as the park—and although she seemed proud of our classicist, I imagine Mutti enforced a curfew on his concerts.

Saturday mornings were sacred in the apartment. My father sat for hours at a time, directly in front of our old Philco table model radio, entranced by world-class operas sung by renowned artists at the New York Metropolitan Opera. He ignored the sputtering sounds of the old radio and hummed softly along, ably providing many of the lyrics. Mutti and I sometimes joined him for these long mornings. I vividly remember the soft and measured voice of the famed announcer of the day, Milton J. Cross, as he narrated the various scenes and arias. My favorite, *Hansel and Gretel*, was broadcast every year, two weeks before Christmas. Milton Cross described the beautiful scenes so clearly that I could hold those pictures of the children and the forest in my mind from year to year.

Papa's interests stretched to sports too, and he introduced me to the world of baseball, an element of American culture he could appreciate. Despite its weather, DC summer claimed a great redeeming feature: baseball. The sport of the people, it was the entertainment for DC families, even ours, and prices were scaled to fill the stands with all ages. I am sure that Papa's interest in the sport was whetted by the fact that he met many major league teams when they came to play our Washington Senators. The visiting teams were regular guests of the hotel and known to prefer "Carl's table" in the dining room. Papa understood the game exceptionally well, and according to him the players were grateful for his insights. He admitted to disliking certain players, though, because of what he considered their crude behavior, branding them "uneducated boors" and "tobacco-chewing hillbillies." He had an owner's pride in his hotel: he believed people with poor manners did not belong in such a fine establishment. I was only nine or ten years old, but I could already see that these men were great players despite their lack of refinement and kept my opinion to myself.

Papa had a special place in his heart for two players—Lou Gehrig and Joe DiMaggio, both with the New York Yankees—and I shared his adulation. According to Papa, these men were always "real gentlemen" when they were in the hotel. I didn't realize it then, but when we went to the games, we were watching the historical cream of the baseball crop. Besides these two favorite players, we frequently saw "The Babe" Ruth, Ted Williams, and Jimmy Foxx in their best years. A pavilion seat in the grandstand behind third base cost Papa seventy-five cents, and as a child I was admitted free. If we were really watching our pennies, Papa and I sat in the bleachers at a total cost of twenty-five cents. When our team played home games on Fridays, ladies were admitted free and Mutti joined us.

My father was also an avid fisherman who never let living in the city interfere with his sport. On a number of occasions, he and a half dozen or so of his friends from work would split the twenty-dollar cost of a boat and its captain, and take me along for a day's fishing on Chesapeake Bay. I had a price to pay, though, for my boat ride: collecting night crawlers for bait. The night before the trip, a friend and I, flashlights in hand, would sneak up on those fat rascals stretched out in the cool night grass of the local city park. After an hour or two, we usually had a hundred or more worms stored in a big coffee can, ready for the next day's outing. On a good day we had fish for dinner.

Fisherman, baseball fan, dramatist, chef, self-educated man—this was the side of Papa I admired and respected all my life. The other side of Papa, the one who persistently plunged our family into financial ruin and drank late into the night with his friends at the Speakeasies and shrugged off responsibilities, was the one who paled in comparison.

twelve

The Great Depression Begins

Washington, DC

1930s

In a cruel twist, in the early part of the decade, the Prohibition Era had not yet ended when the Great Depression began. I was nine years old. I had no way of knowing that our nation's homes and family-owned farms were being lost to foreclosure, that families were being broken, that jobs for over fifteen million people were disappearing. I credit my parents for shielding me from much of this national pain. Only as the long ordeal persisted did I begin to feel that much of life had changed.

I later learned that thousands of workers, once employed in well-paying jobs, were reduced to menial work. In large cities like ours, some tried to eke out a living as part-time laborers; others sold newspapers and apples for pennies on busy street corners. Those who had any regular employment at all were considered fortunate, as many were reduced to standing in welfare lines for food that would let them survive each day. Still, the nation was only at the beginning of a crisis that was to last ten long years before staggering into another catastrophe—World War II.

It was not long before the Great Depression, like the Prohibition era before it, was felt directly in our little apartment. It was no small wonder that Mutti became even more exasperated than usual with Papa. She had clear memories of the poverty and desperation of her childhood in Germany between the Wars. Papa had been sheltered from abject poverty from age fourteen, roaming the world on freighters or passenger ships, and enjoying exotic ports, secure housing and meals, and the fellowship of crewmates. And so he continued, as he always had, to spend a portion of his increasingly meager earnings on his nightly visit to the speakeasy. The fact that fewer and fewer patrons were coming to the hotel seemed not to bother him.

I had no understanding of the depth of crisis our country faced, and little awareness that our family's usual problems with money had greatly escalated. There is an advantage to living in a poor neighborhood: there are no Joneses to keep up with, no basis for comparison, and in those days, no televised images to envy. Everyone I knew was in the same dilemma, and as a child I thought this was normal. We had never been the kind of kids who bought new clothes in the big stores downtown or purchased shoes that fit in a real shoe store, so I was not aware of any serious lack in my daily life. After all, I had sports equipment—bats made of broomsticks, old tennis balls, and footballs made from tightly wadded newspapers tied with string. All of my buddies were in the same fix and treasured our makeshift gear.

Papa explained to me that there were big advantages to being poor. We could not lose anything of value because we never owned anything of value. We had no home or car that could be repossessed. We had never gotten far enough ahead to make a down payment on anything costly, not even the refrigerator that Mutti kept begging for.

Years later, Mutti told me how her view of finances differed from Papa's. I am sure she was afraid I would take his economics lessons to heart and live my life as a pauper. "He is unwilling to accept responsibility or debt of any kind," she told me. While my parents' friends had been gradually leaving our neighborhood and putting down payments on modest homes and practical cars, we went on paying our rent and bus fares. She explained that Papa did not believe in savings, nor in mortgages and loans. He reasoned that those responsibilities would cause worry, interfering with his enjoyment of life and his need to have cash at the ready for entertaining his friends.

Papa's theory put our family in financial bondage all our lives, but especially in the midst of the Depression. He insisted we had no need to live in "fancy neighborhoods" and steadfastly refused promotions at work to headwaiter or dining manager. Those positions, he insisted, only brought trouble and worry. Ironically, the Depression claimed many homes and cars of our friends, leaving Mutti without an air-tight argument for loans and mortgages.

As the 30s went on, I gradually became aware that my parents were reaching a crisis point, having an unusually hard time getting sufficient money together for food, utilities, and rent. Mutti had been doing part-time housekeeping work; no full-time employment was ever available, and it took some adjustment of thinking on Papa's part to allow his German wife to work outside the home.

As long as I could remember, paying bills was a stressful time of the month. Our apartments were always small, but with each move we managed to squeeze in our old oak table that could serve as kitchen counter, dining room, and bookkeeping center. Mutti would sit at the table, notebooks spread open, one for each bill, jotting notes and erasing them, then jotting again until she had selected the most critical to pay, or partially pay, that month. The difference now was that she closed the notebooks faster. With no savings, she would merely shrug and say, "There's no good answer."

Tips at the hotel eventually decreased to the point that even Papa looked worried, and he seemed to make some effort to conserve. Though he started coming home earlier, he and Mutti resumed their late night/early morning arguments. These "discussions" had a quieter tone than they had before, more serious, perhaps more deliberative. Hard decisions hung in the air. I'd been falling asleep early each night after long days of school and baseball play, but I sensed it was time for vigilance, so Barrie and I would carefully listen.

One night during my vigils, I learned that we could no longer pay the rent. We had moved one or two times recently, looking for cheaper quarters, but even this modest apartment was not cheap enough. Papa and Mutti decided to break up our home until things got better, so we packed up a few clothes and cleaned the apartment for new tenants. Mutti put furniture of even minimal value into storage and sold the rest for whatever cash she could retrieve.

The plan was that Papa would join two of his friends from the hotel to work in Canada for a time while I stayed back with Mutti. The impact of the Depression was not as evident in that country, and work was available in luxury hotels since Prohibition was not in effect there. This combination of advantages had encouraged many Americans who still had some semblance of wealth to live comfortably in the neighboring country, and they would stay through the Depression free of most of the troubles that plagued their own nation.

Strangely, I don't have any memory of Papa's leaving us, nor any sense of this being a traumatic separation as a family. Perhaps my parents took such care to make this a positive move that I never retained any memory, yet I also know that as a toddler there were many such separations from my father, few of which still rest in my mind.

After crossing the Canadian border, Father and his two friends easily found desirable positions in the city of Quebec, becoming waiters at the world-famous Hotel Chateau de Frontenac. It seemed to have been a sound plan at the time, but Papa's immigration to Canada would in the future have serious consequences for him and for our family, leaving Papa's risk-taking to follow us again.

For the time being, Mutti answered a small ad and secured employment as a cook on a large Virginia farm owned by the Branstetter family. Mr. Branstetter farmed a huge tract of over a thousand acres and had hired eight to ten additional hands to work the crops in the coming growing season. The large farm was located some twenty miles from Manassas, the site of two famous Civil War battles—the Battle of Bull Run in 1862, and two years later, the Second Manassas.

Mutti's job was to cook three meals a day, seven days a week, for over twenty farmhands. She had some assistance from the farmer's wife and his older daughter, but hers was truly a full-time job. The farmer had two sons, Max who was about my age, and Joe who was three years older. The three of us had a fine time. I do not recall that we were ever expected to do much in the way of work around the farm, other than feeding the free-roaming chickens, slopping the hogs, and bringing in the cows each evening—chores that were always more fun than work for me.

During that first summer, I also made friends with Jim Moss, who was my age and lived on a smaller farm next to the one where we were staying. We had great times together exploring all the nooks and crannies of old abandoned farmhouses that now were home only to families of mice. We captured them by designing our own live traps and attempted to train our prisoners to do simple tricks.

Another entertainment was capturing June bugs (large flying beetles), upon whose legs we would tie a tiny thread that became a "leash" allowing us to control their direction of flight. Ultimately, we would release them and seek new adventures.

It was a perfect life for a ten-year-old city boy. As amateur archeologists we hunted for arrowheads in newly turned fields, and skinny-dipped on hot summer afternoons by diving into the Bull Run, which bordered the farm on the southern boundary. Catfish and bass as well as wary water turtles abounded in the lazy stream. The turtles let us get just close enough to see their beautifully striped heads before they splashed off the log into the muddy waters of the Run. From time to time, we spied garter snakes around the edges of the fields, along with feared water moccasins gliding easily through the water.

Jim had a little sister Dorothy, who was about seven and just old enough to pester us whenever the opportunity arose. She had a pet chicken, which for some unknown reason failed to grow any feathers or get any larger than a pullet. It was fun to watch because it acted more like a dog than a chicken. Named "Baldy," the chicken was Dorothy's devoted pet, sitting in her lap, eating corn kernels out of her hand, and running close behind her whenever we felt the need to chase her.

We rarely saw much of Jim's older brother, about eighteen by then, because he had both a part-time job on the farm next door and a heavy crush on that family's daughter. Whenever he was around, he gave us a hard time as older boys are wont to do, and we teased him right back about making out with the farmer's daughter.

Summer on the farm ended too quickly and soon it was mid-

September. Mutti and I returned to Washington to face school for me and a new job for her. Our new apartment was even smaller than the last but, happily for me, in our old neighborhood. My friends and I played baseball, and Mother took a position as housekeeper and childcare provider for a moderately situated family living in the suburbs of Washington. Unlike the nation's typical family at that time, the man of the house was connected with the film industry, and his wife worked for the government, so they could afford such an arrangement.

When Papa returned from Canada, he took a new job at the deluxe Carlton Hotel in downtown Washington, but like other workers in this era, his and Mutti's wages were greatly depressed. It was still a struggle for my family to make a go of it, even now with a second income. But those sunny days on the farms, skinny-dipping in the Bull Run, catching frogs, salamanders, and garter snakes in the boggy lower fields, trying to hunt a rabbit now and then with our trusty homemade slingshots (we never got one)—all of this left me with a wonderful mental scrapbook of memories that carried me through the cold and dreary winter days that lay ahead.

thirteen

More Years of Adapting

1934

I'll never forget the day President Franklin Roosevelt sent us a refrigerator. I had heard him on the radio week after week, and I believed in his promises to the nation. I didn't exactly pray to him, but it was close. Although money and jobs were still scarce, a sense of optimism permeated our lower-middle-class neighborhood—Franklin Delano Roosevelt was going to make things better.

By now, small electric refrigerators were common—just not in our home. Every three days an iceman lifted a huge fifty-pound chunk of ice to his shoulder, hefted it up two flights of stairs to our apartment, then wrestled it into the icebox. In summer, the ice inside it simply melted. Nothing could stand up against DC's July and August.

Mutti had been talking about a refrigerator for as long as I could remember, but we could never afford one. Acquiring the cheapest model would cost a little over one hundred dollars, which meant taking out a loan and going into debt for the first time.

Papa had for years argued against going into this kind of debt, but for once Mutti stood her ground, and the day finally arrived that we took out a three-year, one-hundred-dollar loan to pay gradually for the gleaming white beauty.

The Great Depression was to last ten years. Like our neighbors and friends, we learned a lot over those years about adapting and making do. Mutti and Papa were exceptionally creative in finding a way to stretch the food budget and have daylong entertainment besides. The three of us often went crabbing on Chesapeake Bay during the summer months, beginning the journey on a small steam train from Washington station through a portion of Maryland, then heading through the countryside toward North Beach. Once at the shore, we walked to the end of the pier, a half-mile jaunt, where we put ten or twelve lines of twine into the sea, each with a chunk of rotten beef tied to it.

When one of the lines moved away and tightened, Mutti would call to Papa and me, then slowly bring it up to the surface, the crab voraciously feeding on the bait. Either Papa or I brought our long-handled dip net up and under him, scooping him out of the Bay and depositing him, fighting all the while, into our huge burlap bag. By the end of the day, we could net forty or fifty pounds of crab.

Ignoring our tiredness from the exercise, we would trudge back to the train station, Papa and I struggling to haul the sack filled with active Chesapeake "Blues" onto the rear train car platform. The live feisty crabs often had their own plan, so one of us stood guard on the platform to control any creature sticking limbs through burlap. Fellow train passengers seemed interested but not surprised: these times called for creativity.

The adventure began in earnest once we reached home, where we had to dump the rascals into the bathtub filled with cold water. We rinsed off mud and seaweed in preparation for the cookpot—a large oval copper washtub that Mutti put on the stove to boil our weekly laundry. Papa and I had the touchy job of conveying the angry crabs from the bathtub into the laundry tub without getting our fingers lacerated in the process. To let our guard down momentarily was to our peril—and we had scars to prove it.

Once cooked, the delicious meat fed us for about a week, as whole chunks, deviled, cakes, and salads. It is hard to believe now, but such an excursion for the whole day, including the forty-mile round-trip train ticket for three of us, cost less than three or four dollars. This happier side of the Great Depression still conjures up fond memories and reminds me of the exuberance and joy of my Papa.

One year, as my summer vacation grew closer, I was mourning the fact that Mutti had a routine job and would not cook at the farm that summer. Like her, I would be confined to the city. In the midst of my moaning, Mutti opened a letter inviting me to come for three weeks to the small Moss Farm in Virginia, adjacent to where she and I had spent the previous summer.

Jim and I picked up where we left off the year before, alternating farm chores with exploration. At thirteen, we were able to help Mr. Moss more with the farm work, including the building of a new barn. I don't know how much real help we were, but we thoroughly enjoyed the experience. One day, the two of us drove the team of sturdy farm horses over narrow country lanes to a forested area. Mr. Moss had purchased the rights to fell some trees to use for a framing structure for the main beams of his new barn. He paid us each fifteen cents for our day's "work," and we itched to spend it all in one wild spree buying small fireworks and penny candies at the tiny general store in Bristow.

Mr. Moss was a different kind of father, a kind and patient man who spoke in a soft voice but with authority. He treated me like his own son. Almost seventy years later, I still remember him vividly and fondly. One of his special treats on warm summer evenings was to organize an eggnog party. The drink was made of fresh farm eggs, several quarts of that day's milk heavy with cream, a bit of sugar, and our choice of lemon, vanilla, or orange extract for zest. Mrs. Moss would crank the whole batch together for ten or fifteen minutes in the butter churn (there were no electric mixers; in fact, there was no electricity), and after everybody had their fill, we happily made our way up the creaky staircase to the bedrooms by light of the kerosene lamps. The ritual before going to sleep was reading the latest Sears Roebuck catalog by lamplight, checking out the .22 caliber rifles, pistols, and ammunition, and especially the bras and girdles that the pretty models were showing those days. My going to Virginia to live with the Moss family another summer was a highlight of those years, and it was yet another way my parents' creativity helped me survive the sorrow of the city.

Sadly, later the following year, we learned the Moss family had lost their farmhouse and land, including the new barn and the team of work horses. They had not been able to keep up monthly mortgage payments and eventually faced foreclosure and even eviction. This was not an infrequent story in those grim days; farm families seemed to be more victimized than city dwellers. Though my family visited the Mosses several times after they moved to Washington, it never felt right to see them in a tiny gray walk-up apartment, far from their beautiful farm.

All set to begin junior high, I had grown old enough to see more of what was happening around me in my city and in my own home. We moved again that summer, this time to a commercial downtown zone where public buses were plentiful. I never thought about it at the time, but looking back it seems we were always moving, either avoiding rent increases or needing different public transportation lines. My new school was at a distance from the last apartment, and both Papa and Mutti had new jobs to reach. Although it was a "marginal" area, we had no choice but to live on a bus line.

Some of our family friends were also moving out of the neighborhood, but in contrast to us, they were "moving up." They purchased small modest homes, often highly mortgaged and always at some distance from the city. Our buying a refrigerator on a three-year installment plan was as far as Papa could reach in his economic theories. Some things had not changed.

Still, I was spared any real sense of foreboding, probably

because my mother was working outside our home and added a second income to our family till. Without that steady money, surely my home life would have been broken, as I doubt my father would have ever mended his ways of spending and drinking.

Looking back now, I see that another force was changing our lives: our family friends were disappearing. Over the years, Papa and Mutti prepared all week long for their monthly Sunday afternoon visits, finding and cooking the perfect meat for sauerbraten, frosting one of Mutti's renowned cream cakes, squeezing folding chairs around the table. Papa practiced his classical German poetry, and I rehearsed the simple stanzas he assigned me for our after-dinner recitations. As the guests came into the apartment, Wagner's more subdued choruses played. But things had begun to unravel. Each Sunday as the eating and drinking went on, conversations about the state of Germany grew more and more intense. Papa was by far the loudest and most upset.

"How can you say the Germans are doing wrong?" he'd say. "Look at the wrong that was done to them. It was evil, their punishment after the Great War."

My father's intensity apparently grew too strong even for our German friends to accept. One Sunday morning I saw only four place settings being prepared at the table—not our usual eight or nine. Before long, Papa's German poetry recitals grew less frequent and his audiences smaller. Some who no longer came now lived too far away for the evening excursions to our apartment—but distance alone did not account for all who were missing. They had been kind and encouraging to me, and I wished they were there.

Either German or Austrian born, they had been eager to keep the culture of the homeland alive—until they weren't.

It wasn't until my adult years that I came to understand our friends had begun to change loyalties, even going so far as to begin the process of becoming US citizens. Papa was appalled at what he saw as their rejection of the homeland, and our world in the apartment started to shrink.

fourteen

Turmoil Everywhere

Washington, DC

1934

This particular year was riddled with turmoil—in the nation where families were still battling the Depression, in our apartment where Papa grew more and more agitated over Germany's needs, and in my school where the hormones of adolescents collided daily.

In our new neighborhood of mixed commercial and residential units, we lived on the third floor toward the back of a large building, where the clamor from the street was mostly blocked. The local bus stopped noisily right at our building door, though. For a dollar fifty a month, I bought the forty tickets I needed to ride to and from school. Today that amount sounds trivial, but it was significant in those days. Each month, I hesitated to remind Mutti of the fare that was due. It was a dollar fifty that could have been added to our food budget, but, hiding her anxiety well, she never pointed that out.

Father and Son

It was the prior year, when I was twelve, that I realized if I wanted to enjoy some of the pleasant "extras" of life—the occasional Saturday movie or a popular comic book—I would have to start a career. I had heard our adult friends talk about their careers and it seemed clear: I needed one, particularly now for my school bus fare. I was a teenager now, after all, and I aimed to be more self-sufficient.

I started my business endeavors as a newspaper salesman. I didn't have an office, but I did have a well-constructed wooden wagon with specially made steel-rimmed tires. It was purchased on a three-month payback plan from the *Washington Evening Star*, one of the city's more prestigious and refined papers. The newspaper's name was emblazoned in red along the sides of the wagon. Very classy. I believed I was the envy of other carriers across the city, most of whom carried their papers in cheap canvas bags.

Six days a week, I delivered about sixty-five morning papers to homes outside my neighborhood. In our block of houses, having your own newspaper was a luxury. My parents, like others who lived near us, usually stood once a day near the corner newsboy and listened while he belted out the headlines, none of which varied much day to day: "More Jobs Lost!" "City Bank Closes!"

Every Sunday, I regretted my job choice. One hundred heavy weekend editions arrived at my curb by five a.m. and took at least three hours to deliver. Snowy Sundays meant borrowing a sled and doubling the time for pulling deliveries up icy roads. Worse yet, on the last Sunday of the month, I had to travel to my crotchety old boss's apartment to deliver his profits. He began his drinking early in the morning, and by the time I arrived, he barely saw me through red eyes. His math skills deteriorated by the hour, and every month there was a lengthy discussion about what was due him. Finally, perhaps getting "thirsty," he would agree with my calculations.

This job became a tough way to learn about the Depression. Mutti and Papa continued to make the most of our lives, but I was beginning to see just how much reality they had to be hiding from me. It wasn't just the newspaper headlines that educated me, it was the families who moved out in the night, leaving landlords—and newsboys—stranded without pay.

Despite the hardships, I kept my enterprise going for about a year. At an average of seventeen dollars a month, it was good money for a young teenager. Best of all, I never had to put the tap on Mutti for extra funds. That felt good, but it felt even better to sell my used wagon to a new newsboy when the job came to a close for me.

The next three years held the most unhappy and unsettling experiences of my life as an older child, in large part because junior high seemed a time to label each others' differences. I was teased for my lingering German accent and nicknamed "Dutch," the German boy who came from the poorest part of the city. The school structure demanded a difficult adjustment; not having a single teacher for all subjects was startling and frustrating for me. I was an only child who still flourished under strong relationships and needed the guidance of adults, yet I found little warmth from my teachers. Teaching nearly one hundred and fifty students a day probably contributed to that, and I wasn't much of a student anyway. I continued to struggle with language, particularly written assignments and essay writing. Though I was developing some talent in the arts, particularly painting and drawing, no one seemed to notice.

As if academics were not enough challenge, ongoing physical changes of puberty had me so mixed up that I was in constant inner and outer turmoil. I was trying to be a "grownup" one day and the next day I was a little kid again. My altercations with other boys who were probably just as mixed up as I was got me sent at least twice a week to detention and earned me several visits to the vice-principal's office each month. I provoked some pretty tense times at home when report cards came out too. Papa would make his agitation known by reading more and more loudly from his German newspapers. To add further insult, school authorities called my parents on multiple occasions about "my terrible attitude and lack of cooperation."

At the same time, independent from my school behavior, home was becoming more and more stressful. In this case the combination of my unhappiness at school and Papa's anger at what he saw as the neglect of Germany sometimes escalated into a yelling match between us. Luckily, Mutti would quickly intervene. And we all felt the sadness of having fewer of our immigrant friends come to dinner on weekend nights. I missed them, their courtly European manners, and their interest in my life—my life that was currently miserable wherever I turned.

As I got older and talked with other men about this period in their own lives, I found my experience in junior high wasn't all that unusual: most of the men had had similar, or worse, trouble during those middle school years, caught between childhood and adolescence. In later life, when I became a school administrator, I was occasionally offered the principalship of a junior high school. I would politely decline the offer, all the while resisting my impulse to run and scream. I had listened with some amusement to the horror stories of my colleagues who had the misfortune to be involved with this age group on a daily basis—and they didn't distinguish between boys and girls. According to them, those poor souls, like I had been, were *all* trouble from ages twelve to fifteen.

fifteen

Growing Up in DC

On Easter, I was one of those children who rolled colorfully dyed eggs down the White House lawn. As a teenager, each July fourth I waited in line with my friends at the National Mall, hoping for prime seats at the night celebration. At Christmas I held my breath in amazement as the capitol area lights were turned on, strand by strand. My buddies and I staged after-school foot races and softball games on the grassy National Mall, then visited the Lincoln Memorial either seeking solace or sharing jubilation. We grew used to seeing President Roosevelt's motorcade driving past us on the way to the White House, waiting for his familiar smile and wave. And in good weather, DC hosted bands and parades from across the region. We would hear the musicians warming up and race each other to a front-row curb seat.

Growing up in the District of Columbia had many magical moments, although at the time, having nothing to compare, I never realized the moments were magical. I assumed everyone lived this kind of life. DC was simply my hometown, my neighborhood. I never imagined that before long, tens of thousands of people would flood this place once there was a war to fight.

As a child and teenager, I had grown accustomed to the ways the life of my family, poor and powerless as it was, touched the lives of the powerful and wealthy of the city. Papa served J. Edgar Hoover his daily lunch and shared baseball tips with Joe DiMaggio. He knew FBI agents and senators by their first names. I once had a job in a luxury hotel, running an elevator that ferried congressmen and their call girls to the penthouse floor. Mutti had a part-time job readying Kathryn Graham's caboose car for excursions, cherishing the few but warm encounters with the *Washington Post* owner. "It gleams," Ms. Graham would say, and Mutti would gleam when she told us of the praise.

My Uncle Carl, himself a native of Austria, was resident butler and head of staff at the Czechoslovakian Embassy. Ordinarily that was a role requiring only polished European manners, a stiffly starched tuxedo, and an ability to keep young employees in line. But when Germany invaded Czechoslovakia, Uncle Carl was directed to raise the Nazi flag over the Embassy in DC. The next morning, my uncle's picture was on the front page of nearly every major newspaper, some of which noted that his Austrian heritage was shared with Hitler.

It is likely, however, that Aunt Nettel knew the most significant secret of all.

Working as head housekeeper for an extraordinarily wealthy family, she had two charges: a toddler who easily won her heart, and his mother, a young and vibrant widow who was also a beautiful and lively socialite. The young woman's husband had been a famous artist in DC, and after his death she began an affair with a married Supreme Court justice. Neither the justice nor the socialite were known for their discretion, but on one more secretive trip, they drove cross-country with the little boy and his nanny, Aunt Nettel, all the way to Washington state where they occupied a remote forested lodge for several days.

Shortly before my graduation from junior high school, my father showed Mutti and me a yet-unopened formal-looking white envelope, its return address an apartment in New York City. It was rare that we received mail other than bills and letters from the homeland, and Papa said that he and Mutti would open it first. They went into their bedroom and shut the door behind them. Apparently, there had been much to discuss between them because the minutes stretched to an hour before they emerged.

The letter was from a Mr. Hirsch who lived in New York City. He wished to meet me and to treat me to what he called "the finer things of the city." Papa seemed at a loss to explain just who this Mr. Hirsch was, but said that he had met him about fifteen years ago and that he seemed a fine man. He must, Papa said, be quite elderly now. I assumed he was some long-lost grandfather or uncle. Other than Aunt Nettel, I had never met older relatives, and having one invite me to New York seemed just fine to me. Neither Papa nor Mutti told me any more about who he might be, and Papa said he would have to think about the invitation for a few days. No doubt this was because Mr. Hirsch's former wife Francesca, became my mother after Papa lured her away from him. Surely, he and Mutti had no desire to recount the details of that romance.

I remember every minute of my week in New York. Everything was a contrast to how my family lived. Looking back now as an adult, I ponder the difference between the luxurious life Mr. Hirsch offered my birth mother Francesca, and the vagabond but passionate existence Papa must have given her. She had chosen Papa, but then his magnetism and charisma often drew people to him.

Mr. Hirsch had thought of every detail for my visit, even sending me a first-class train ticket. Clutching my small case, I was surrounded by business men in suits carrying briefcases, looking at me curiously. I was embarrassed when I realized my school pants and flannel shirt were not New York City garb.

As I stepped off the train into the sprawling station, I experienced the panic of a new traveler: *What if he forgets me? What if he's changed his mind and doesn't want me?*

I had only a few minutes to worry because a man dressed in a chauffeur uniform called my name loudly. He said we would fetch the rest of my luggage at the baggage claim. I wasn't sure how to tell him that what he saw was what I had, but lucky for me, he was quick to understand.

"Tell you what, son, Mr. Hirsch loves to go shopping. You'll be leaving here with all kinds of new cases. Just you see."

Father and Son

A tall and thin, rather bent-over gray-haired gentleman dressed in a dark navy suit, got out of the car to shake my hand in greeting. I immediately noticed how soft his voice was. I settled into the back seat next to him for the first leg of my adventure.

Mr. Hirsch's apartment was large and luxurious, unlike anything I had ever seen. We didn't spend much time there, though—he had plans for us to visit museums, attend concerts, and enjoy dinners out with his friends. He seemed so proud to introduce me, which to this day I don't quite understand. Just exactly how had he explained me? In the meantime, I thought of him as a grandfather. My friends all had at least one grandfather, and I had always wished I had one too.

And the shopping—the driver was so right. Mr. Hirsch relished seeing the latest and best of the stores in the city. After buying me several practical outfits for school, he insisted we go to the leading tailor on Fifth Avenue, pick out a light wool fabric, and have a suit made just for me for my graduation. Mutti had always made our clothes, but I knew this was a new ball game. In my class picture taken later that year, I am sitting in the front row, smiling broadly, proudly displaying my first-class suit.

There was another reason for my smile: I was finally moving on to high school in the fall. Junior high had been the most challenging part of my life so far, and even I had been shocked that I could get my behavior well enough under control to graduate that year. I had no idea what awaited me in the years to come, and I was both trepidatious and eager to find out.

sixteen

Old Friends, New Friends

Washington, DC

I continued to miss our German friends. They had always been kind to me, encouraging me to do well despite the odds and taking a strong interest in my Boy Scout troop. The Scouts were a bit too American for Papa's taste. He didn't forbid my taking part but neither did he come to ceremonies and activities. In contrast, Mutti sat proudly through each of my award ceremonies.

Scout uniforms cost a prohibitive seventeen dollars. But asking around, I learned a uniform was not technically required to join. The leader told me I only had to buy the first part of the outfit, the fifty-cent neckerchief. That got me in the door of Troop 45 as a charter member in its newly formed fourth unit, the Black Panther Patrol (no relationship to the Black Panthers of decades later).

Scouting was a big-time adventure for raunchy immigrant kids like us. It became a strong guiding force for our early teen years, bringing us into close contact with kids from different backgrounds and races. Up until the Scouting experience, German and Austrian teens in our neighborhood and school had pretty much clung together, and an experience with Papa and his prejudices a few years earlier had taught me not to talk at home about playing with Negro children. When I was about ten, Papa learned that a black youngster and I often played ball together, then he plopped me into the bathtub and scrubbed me harshly with a bristle brush and strong laundry soap until my body turned stinging cherry red. He made his point: he would scrub the other child's influence off me anytime it was necessary.

Those of Jewish heritage were considered persona non grata to Papa too, a position taken by many Americans during these pre-war years. Besides trying to restrict me from black children, Papa insisted that Mutti and I avoid anyone Jewish. She and I ignored his edict, but cities throughout America began to allow private clubs and institutions to hang large signs that read "No Jews Allowed." Decades later, such race and religious intolerances have lessened, but still we cannot claim that these problems have been totally erased. My personal feeling is that it will be at least two more generations before this type of intolerance will disappear.

I stayed with scouting—still proudly wearing my neckerchief as uniform—for a few years. I was able to earn a number of the required merit badges to reach the "Life" level, only one notch below the pinnacle of "Eagle." These badges had much to do with outdoor prowess and skill, and they could hardly be completed if you never got out of the city. DC kids didn't have a chance when it came to earning badges in canoeing, water life-saving, outdoor cooking, outdoor mapping, and tracking. But Scout leaders were adaptive: they placed all of these achievements within our reach at three-week camp sessions each summer.

Camp was a great experience, complementing in a meaningful and structured way experiences I had had on Mr. Moss's Virginia farm. Our troops camped on two hundred acres at Plum Point on the shores of the Chesapeake Bay. By taking a job as KP (Kitchen Police), I earned a couple of extra weeks room and board each summer, at no cost to my family. KP was a tough job, though. A scout master wakened us at four thirty each morning to set up, serve, and clean up after the breakfast meal for two hundred other scouts. That was the routine for all three meals every day except Sunday noon, when the whole camp ate out, picnic style, on the beach. Between work shifts in the mess hall, I usually had five or six hours free each day when I could work on my merit badges.

At the end of that last camp experience, I started my freshman year and lost motivation for scouting. As a result, I never did begin the work toward an Eagle badge.

I was now nearly fifteen and a new life had begun to emerge for me in the neighborhood. I had two good friends who lived within blocks of my apartment house, and although we attended different high schools, we saw each other daily. Despite coming from different ethnic backgrounds, we became fast friends. Jim

Father and Son

Chumas was the son of a first-generation Greek family, and Jesse D'Alosio was an only child from a first-generation Italian family. Both lived in virtually non-English-speaking homes, whereas my parents and I spoke only English, apart from rare occasions with German friends or relatives, and even more rare when only the three of us were home. In later years, I lamented that my German language skills were quickly replaced by English; as I grew into adulthood, I realized I had lost something that could have enriched my later life and travels.

In contrast to me, Jim was sent to Greek language school three times a week after his regular public school classes in order to maintain his cultural roots, language, and friends. Jesse attended no cultural school, but as an only child, he was often put in the position of being a translator for his parents who spoke only broken English and did not read the language easily. The three of us accepted these differences among ourselves without any special attention or comment and greatly enjoyed distinct family meals in each other's homes. I still remember those spicy and pungent Italian and Greek dinners, but because of the language barrier, there was little social contact among any of the adults.

Jesse's father was an expert tailor for a prestigious men's clothing firm in downtown Washington, and his mother was a homemaker. Jim's father owned The Moderne Restaurant, a modest neighborhood café with its elegant name boldly printed in large gold letters on its front window. The name—which hadn't been changed since Jim's father and uncle bought the place fifteen years earlier—didn't reflect the interior at all. It was true Americana, including a small soda fountain with a four-seater bar for Cokes and shakes. Later, when Prohibition ended, the soda counter was removed and eight or ten booths were installed in its place. The cafe quickly became the neighborhood tavern, serving a unique and colorful clientele that ranged from prosperous realtors who occupied the office next door, to cab drivers, bookies, prostitutes, and a variety of lower-level government workers.

Washington had many sheltered, safe, and beautiful residential areas for its upper middle class, neighborhoods made up of single homes or well-kept row houses primarily in the northwest and northeast sections of Washington—but that's not where we lived. Those houses might have been nicer than ours, but I wonder if those who lived in that well-regulated north side had the colorful days (and nights) we had. Being pretty savvy to the ways of the world by this time, the three of us made sure that what we saw and what we knew about in our environment never found its way into dinner table conversations with our parents.

Jesse, Jim, and I had our favorite regular hangouts that each contributed to our urban education. Not surprisingly, Jim's family restaurant was our first choice. Besides its wonderfully interesting patrons, it had lively pinball machines and even a public telephone (not too often seen in those days). From about age twelve, Jim had worked regularly at the restaurant, typing the menus for the next day's offerings and making sandwiches after school hours. Jesse and I hung close by, becoming steady "sharks" on the pinball machine and winning many free games, which were turned into credit toward meals or anything else we wanted from the restaurant.

Another favored hangout was Hoover's Florist just down the street from the restaurant. The flower shop was our summertime favorite because Mr. Hoover always kept the radio broadcast on for the Washington Senators' baseball games, and he joined us in cheering on those far too few occasions of a good play. The florist, in addition to giving us many hours for loafing and listening to ball games, also gave the three of us opportunity to travel about the city in the oversized delivery truck. For funerals or weddings, the florist rented out potted palms and we helped George, the black driver, carry them from the funeral parlor or church to the cemetery or reception hall. We rode for hours all over DC delivering flowers, wreaths, and plants. We not only learned every street, avenue, and alley in the city, but we also gained valuable knowledge from the detailed analysis George offered of his amazing romantic encounters the night before.

Mr. Hoover also had a son, Lou, who was around twenty-two. He was athletic and strong, and he would take us on two at a time to see if we could hold him down or vice versa. He drove an almost new, 1935 convertible Ford touring car, and the four of us would pile into it. If Lou was in the mood and had the time, we would grab our baseball gloves and tear down to the Washington Monument grounds (a ten-minute drive), where he would belt high flies with the special fungo bat he used, and the three of us would shag them for an hour or so.

Like many teenagers, we three were seldom home. In my case that was undoubtedly good: Papa and I had fewer chances to conflict over allegiances. As I grew more and more into an

American teen, Papa held tighter to our family being German.

Our neighborhood was peopled with characters that strike me today as coming right out of a Damon Runyon story, particularly *Guys and Dolls*. Most notable was Chisel Chin, the Irish cop who for years walked the neighborhood beat and patrolled our blocks. We kids never wanted to cross him. He was big, burly, and mean, with a chin that jutted out from under his nose like the shelf of a cliff. There were no walkie-talkie radios for cops to use in those days, no squad cars to call except from a special police phone on the corner—just this single cop on the beat, making his rounds at certain hours, changing directions every now and then "just to throw the buggers off."

Chisel Chin knew everything about everybody, and we perceived him as always giving us a hard time in those growing-up years. Our strong defense was to know the pattern of his walk. He always said he would "run us in" if he caught us playing touch football on the Lutheran Church lawn or riding our apple box scooters (with roller skate wheels on the bottom) hell bent in death-defying races from one sidewalk corner to the next. We made sure to wait until he got past certain areas before we would begin or resume our games.

It was common knowledge that Chisel Chin would take advantage of his position as the local "lawman" and help himself to just about anything that struck his appetite or fancy. On cold winter nights, he would frequently slip into the kitchen of Jimmy's family restaurant, hike up his heavy dark-blue overcoat, and whip out a pint flask of Old GrandPapa. He would finish half of it in one long swig, then turn to the black chef to tell him he was ready to eat. He would wolf down his food standing up, then with a satisfied burp, leave the kitchen without so much as a "thanks"—and certainly without paying.

We often saw Chisel Chin on the sidewalks, chatting amiably with Dolly, Sweet Sue, and Millie, the three local "ladies of the night" out scouting for potential customers. Rather than run them in, he was probably lining himself up for a couple bucks of payola or a freebie later that evening.

Then there was old Tony, the short, pudgy shoemaker who had his basement repair shop next door to Hoover's Florist. Among several distinguishing attributes that defined Tony was his bulbous Roman nose covered with multicolored warts. Every Friday night, Tony hustled four or five customers for a little penny ante poker. We would sit around the dining room table in the back room of his shop, learning the refrain of the old saw that you have to "pay the piper when you choose to dance." During the first ten or so hands we played each week, Tony would slip a nickel from the winning pot into his pocket, saying it was "for the house." As the night wore on, Tony served homemade "rot gut red wine" for which he charged ten cents per small jelly glass. By the last hour of the games, with everyone feeling pretty rosy, Tony would start slipping ten cents out of every pot, dropping them into his pocket too. By the time the games ended for the night, I swear Tony had more coins from the money he'd swiped than did the ultimate winner of the evening. We didn't mind the skimming too much, because where else could you drink and gamble without being hauled off to the slammer if you or the house manager got caught? Some nights we could even get lucky and win a buck or two.

Another one of our favorite characters who made himself at home in the restaurant was "Horse Face" Charley Melzer, the on and off again independent cab driver. Horse Face had crafty, deep-set eyes that always darted right and left, an elongated nose to match his pointed chin, and a slouchy fedora pulled over his stringy, oily hair. In fact, without being unkind (because we really liked old Horse Face), he always reminded me of a cornered rat even when he was happy. With his hands in his pockets constantly jangling a bit of loose change, he seemed always to have a "deal," most likely shady and ready to be made at a moment's notice.

When Horse Face wasn't hustling somebody to his cab, he would set up lively crap games in his messy one-room apartment a block or two from our "home base," The Moderne. He knew every cop in the city, it seemed, and he also knew every bookie and numbers runner in our downtown area. You want booze? Girls? A room? Or to lay a bet? Horse Face Charley was your man. Once in a while one of us would ride in the front seat of his cab and listen with fascination to the conversations he conducted with his fares—men, women, young or old, it didn't matter to Horse Face; he jollied them all. After telling a string of outrageous lies about his life and times in the city, he always ended up with a fat tip.

Eddie was another regular at The Moderne. Eddie (we called him Fast Eddie) always claimed to have lost his original business in the Depression. We were never told just what kind of business it was, but we all knew old Fast Eddie as the local "Numbers Man."

Father and Son

One of the biggest scams in the city was the Numbers Game, based on the outcome of the day's horse races at Belmont Park. It brought thousands of illegal gambling dollars into a variety of hands, particularly into those of the "Mob" and of crooked lawmen and politicians on the take. The legitimate odds of winning were about 1,000 to 1, but they actually only paid out 540 to 1, meaning if you had bet a dollar, say, on the winning number and it hit, you would receive $540. The numbers man who sold you the ticket would always pay up immediately, expecting a good tip when he came around the next day with your winnings. Eddie was only a tiny cog in this huge illegal enterprise: there were hundreds like him running their routes five days a week. These guys were merely small operators in a highly lucrative racket run by the big boys, who in turn, worked for the Mafia. They had a ready audience among the financially depressed and the gamblers: who wouldn't venture a nickel or dime on the chance of a nice payoff?

My father played the numbers off and on for twenty years and, as far as I knew, only once hit a winner for $540. He probably never broke even, but that big win was cause for a family celebration. The scam operated on such a blatant level that one can hardly imagine how much payoff there must have been at all levels of law enforcement agencies across the East Coast alone. The numbers game is still in vogue today, prospering around most large cities. The spirit of Fast Eddie lives on.

Our three local "Ladies of the Night" were regulars at The Moderne, though Jim's father was leery about them soliciting their business in his establishment. Dolly was a statuesque black-haired, half-Indian beauty; Millie was a tall, busty blonde; and Sweet Sue was a feisty, petite redhead who possessed all the accoutrements for the trade. The three regularly patronized the restaurant for a beer, a sandwich, or some other kind of quick pickup—being discreet in how they managed their enterprise from the cafe. No matter the weather—snow in winter, humidity in summer—most of their contacts were made standing outside the restaurant. Prostitutes each had their own territory, even their own street corner, and our three did not take kindly to newcomers trading in the neighborhood. They nonetheless did a lot of "street walking" now and then to expand their advertising potential.

Such was life in the neighborhood. High school was a whole other animal.

seventeen

High School

Washington, DC

Ours was not the sort of family that sat leisurely around the kitchen table discussing their child's future, surrounded by college brochures, weighing opportunity against opportunity. Most nights, Papa was likely to be working at the hotel, reading a German newspaper, or joining old sailor friends at a bar. Mutti would be busy preparing the next day's lunch sacks or sewing clothing for us while I would be making a vain attempt to produce a little homework. Our life was centered on today, not on dreams or degrees or careers of tomorrow.

Nonetheless, my big shock had come when, after barely escaping junior high, I began to enjoy my classes at McKinley Technical High School. That enjoyment led to me becoming a better student. I had chosen McKinley Tech because in addition to offering basic subjects required for a diploma and college entrance, it had a wide selection of classes in the manual trades. The school was wonderfully equipped with sophisticated machines, and I quickly saw a good future as a tool and die maker. My major work took place in the machine shop, with collateral courses in drafting, geometry, and metric applications.

An even greater surprise to me and to my parents was that I did well in history and English literature classes, not knowing that someday those interests would point the way to my career choice. By the time I reached my junior year, I maintained a steady pace in my academic classes and barely missed the honor roll by fractions in each of my last four semesters. Chemistry and higher math were my "bugaboos," but considering my past school performance in junior high, to "just miss" the honor roll was a real accomplishment for me.

But my most important learning in those four years came from analyzing the world my successful classmates lived in compared to my own. There was a universe beyond the streets of the city, beyond beat cops, numbers runners, and cabbies. I became aware that there was a clear difference of interests, goals, and behaviors between the chaps in my technical classes (there were no girls in these classes at the time) and the boys and girls I eventually met and befriended in the academically oriented classes.

I made friends easily in both groups but noticed that the students in the academic classes were generally the school leaders and enjoyed popularity among their peers. Besides winning the school's academic awards, most of these students were involved in extracurricular activities, including fraternities, sororities, or the Cadet corps. Many were headed for college after graduation, for by 1937 the intensity of the Depression had begun to subside and many families could begin to look toward a brighter future. I clearly was not in this "in" group, but I did have many close school friends who were.

Unlike my academic friends, my tech classmates were not generally involved with school activities or plans to go on to college; instead, they worked jobs after school, headed for the skilled trades. With my newspaper route and my ice cream delivery business, I fell into this category. This contrast between the tech and academic students led me to my first comprehension of "class stratification" as it existed in my school community. As I became older, it became increasingly evident to me that a solid formal education was the ticket to my being able to compete effectively in the world.

Striving to round out my skill set, I participated in track and football. I never made the first team in football, though, for the simple reasons that I wasn't good enough, heavy enough, tall enough, or motivated enough. Still, practicing every fall afternoon kept me in pretty decent physical condition until indoor track began in January, followed by the outdoor track season in spring. I particularly liked track; my best events were the 100- and 220-yard dashes, where I was able to hold my own among most members of our team. We rarely won inter-city meets with other high schools, but participating forced me into a physical regimen each day. I like to think that it gave me the muscular development and stamina that served me well through most of my adult life.

During my senior year, I suffered a significant setback, one my academic friends would likely never endure. Toothaches were a regular and painful event in my earlier life and continually became worse. Home treatment consisted of applying a hot water bottle and downing two aspirin. When my condition reached the point of almost daily and constant pain, Papa and Mutti decided that I had to see a dentist. This was a big decision, as I had never been to a dentist or doctor of any kind. After sixteen years, it was no surprise that the dentist found I had a mouthful of cavities and was about to lose several molars.

There was no way my parents could afford to pay for this mouthful of problems, but Mutti did a little research and found an ideal solution. All the charges for the work, with the exception of materials, would be waived if I would enroll as a patient of the School of Dentistry at Georgetown University. As a patient, I was given excellent care by graduate students in their last year of dentistry, and all of their work, step by step, was carefully supervised and guaranteed by department heads of the university. The only problem, and it was a minor one considering the alternatives, was that at two visits a week, it would take over five months to finish the repair. Since appointments had to be made after school hours, I lost my place on the track team.

Despite this disappointment, happy and carefree school days continued with final exams, senior year parties and, of course, the major social event of the year: the Senior Prom. For months I'd had my eyes on a little blonde, blue-eyed sweetie from among the junior ranks of the school hierarchy, but I had never asked her for a date. Penny Baardse was pretty much at the top of the girls' social register, but unfortunately, she seemed to prefer dating hefty football heroes. Still, since I had no steady girlfriend, I figured I might as well "shoot for the top." Without a great deal of confidence but with much fake bravado, I popped the big question and was knocked flat when she enthusiastically agreed to be my prom date. Heck, I thought, that was so easy I should have asked her for a date a long time ago! Still, I suspected that the only reason she deemed it appropriate to attend with me was because I had been elected to be the vice president of our graduating class and that we were having our prom at the swank and trendy Shoreham Hotel.

Dear old Uncle Carl came through and loaned me his almost new 1939 Plymouth coupe, complete with radio so we wouldn't need to travel by city bus to the prom. After the ball was over, most of us planned to engage in the requisite bit of spooning in the moonlight before taking our dates home.

It was an extremely cold and icy winter night in January, and even though the moon was shining brightly, driving conditions were hazardous. This fact provided me with a good excuse to pull Uncle Carl's fine car over for a while, listen to the strains of Glenn Miller, and enjoy the moonlight. It all ended too soon after an hour or so when the radio music began to slowly fade and then go out completely. My experience as a driver was limited: it hadn't occurred to me that a six-volt battery supplying the car's system couldn't play a tube-type radio for over an hour in temperatures below freezing and still turn the engine over.

There we sat, dead in the water. Here I had been carefully

cultivating my image all evening as a smooth and charming operator and now my pseudo sophistication melted easily. Penny was pretty calm about all of it because she no doubt had had similar experiences with other dates. She suggested leaving the car and calling a cab, which was a wonderful suggestion had we not been in Rock Creek Park in the middle of DC at 2:00 a.m., with no visible traffic, no gas station in sight, and decades before cell phones had been invented.

The only smart thing I had done all evening—and it was merely dumb luck—was that I had parked on a long and sloping downhill road. I asked Penny to steer while I tried to give the car a nudge away from the curb. Ever so slowly the car began to move. I jumped in and threw it into second gear, turned on the ignition, then gained some good momentum and popped the clutch. The engine caught and away we went. So much for spooning.

One month later, on a cold February night in 1940, with Mutti and Aunt Nettel proudly watching from the audience in our large school auditorium, I received my diploma. Unfortunately, Papa was working and wasn't able to join us. But it was a celebration just the same, exchanging hugs, kisses, and handshakes all around.

It had perhaps never been more apparent that I was an American teenager, not a German teenager. My parents had been US residents for seventeen years, yet neither had even applied for a "Declaration of Intention," a form required to be filed with the Department of Naturalization prior to obtaining full citizenship. Individuals had to be eighteen before they could file this form—and I had just turned eighteen. I had given the decision a lot of thought, and only days earlier, I appeared at the main office of the Department of Naturalization, determined not to tell my parents about this step I had taken toward becoming an American citizen.

Meanwhile, forces that had begun to stir in Europe would shortly change the lives of all of us graduates drastically. A few months earlier, on September 1, 1939, Adolph Hitler and his Nazi forces had invaded Poland, an act triggering an immediate declaration of war against Germany by England and France. The invasions took place almost exactly twenty years from the armistice that was signed with Germany to end World War I. It had been termed the "bloodiest war ever fought in the history of the world," and one the leaders of the victorious allied forces solemnly pronounced it would "end all wars forever."

As the US was not officially involved in the European conflict, all of us naively believed those "foreign affairs" did not much concern us. After our graduation ceremony, a few of us sat on the school steps in our caps and gowns.

"Aren't we lucky?" one of my classmates said.

"Darn right," another responded. "Good thing that's just a war for Europe."

eighteen

Clouds of War

Washington, DC

1941

Living in the nation's capital, we first felt the impact of the European war when we noticed changes within our city neighborhoods. Washington began to hum and bustle far beyond its earlier easygoing pace. The increasing daily commerce and newly created government departments ignited a burst of new residents and workers, along with a long series of office and housing construction projects. What we did not know was that this was just the beginning, a mere trickle of humanity entering our city compared to the massive human tide that was to overwhelm DC in another year or two as the United States itself entered the war.

Permanent residents who had survived in the city during the Depression experienced a slow emergence from economic stagnation to a new level of hope and security for the working man. With my degree in hand from a recognized technical high school and wearing my best jacket, I felt ready to face the world. At this point, any faint idea I had entertained in high school about going to college or getting advanced training had left my mind. I was focused on earning money and getting out on my own.

Both Papa and I became more fixed in our loyalties, and life in our apartment became more and more stressful as the sides of war formed. For example, one evening he and I were listening to the radio when Germany's occupation of France was announced. Papa saw this as positive progress in the war while I, disturbed by the news, left the apartment without a word, determined to find a job and another place to live.

I placed my application with several key industries that were employing trained machinists and apprentices, my primary target being the Washington Navy Yard, located just outside of DC in Virginia. It seemed that in this boom period in DC, I would have my choice of jobs—but that was not to be. Instead, I began to reap the harvest of the decision my father had made many years ago to have his child born in Germany.

Becoming an American citizen required that I be twenty-one years of age, and I was still a German citizen by nationality. In seeking jobs as an apprentice or regular machinist, I consistently reached dead ends. Although my qualifications were high, most companies were currently producing, or planning to produce, military and related defense work. Not surprisingly, they were not willing to consider the employment of someone whose application read:

Country of Birth? GERMANY
City of Birth? HAMBURG
Nationality? GERMAN

Tempting as it was, during these tense times with Germany, I was not about to perjure myself on applications. I was to learn the hard way that my status in the United States would soon officially be termed "Enemy Alien."

My search for work continued for several months until I landed a pretty decent job as a welder's apprentice in a firm not involved in military contract work. I owed this opportunity to the help of my former high school instructor in my Machine Shop major, Emile Schutte, who himself had been a German national and had become an American citizen many years prior. Mr. Schutte gave me an excellent recommendation to a friend who owned a metal fabricating company. Unfortunately, the job did not show much promise, and in less than a year, I was forced to seek out new opportunities.

In the political atmosphere at the time, it seemed apparent that I was not going to get employment in any field commensurate with my training, so I settled—and I mean *really* settled—as an elevator operator in the internationally famous Mayflower Hotel in downtown DC. After several months, I "graduated" from the freight or room service elevator to the main lobby bank of six elevators. Why this renowned hotel would give an enemy alien access to its most prestigious clients, I will never know.

Outfitted in an elaborately adorned red "monkey suit" complete with gold-braided epaulets, white cuffs, a heavily starched white collar, and the crowning glory of a highly stylized pillbox hat, I was quite a sight. But I got free entertainment and nice tips, and I was able to keep track of the comings and goings of the "big wigs" of Washington: senators, congressmen, and foreign dignitaries. I transported many of them up and down with their "girlfriends," some of the most beautiful and highest paid call girls in DC. To be honest, I was far more impressed with meeting the Major League baseball players who also stayed at the Mayflower.

Eventually, I became bored, and in less than six months I got a job as an automotive parts clerk with the largest Chevrolet dealership in the city. I enjoyed this work and began to learn a great deal about the thousands of parts that go into making a car and how each worked. I was earning about fifteen dollars for a 44-hour week, but I was usually broke by the end of it because my "instructor" in the pool parlor across the street charged pretty stiff fees for his "lessons."

In December 1941, America joined England and France and declared war against Germany. This official action had been coming for more than a year, and the attack on Pearl Harbor emphatically pushed the United States into the boiling cauldron of war. DC picked up an even faster pace, with war operations seeming to run on a 24-hour schedule.

Overnight the entire Jensen family became designated "Enemy

Aliens." With that status, an official investigation of our family was initiated by the FBI. We suspected we had been under surveillance for some time—how could anyone miss Papa's diatribes or ignore the fact that he had daily access to J. Edgar Hoover's conversations? After arriving with a warrant, they confiscated the short-wave feature from the radio in our living room, Papa's binoculars from his seafaring days, a hunting knife my Uncle Carl had given me on my seventeenth birthday, and our family's Brownie box camera. Papa was required to sign a release agreement for the removal of these articles, with a promise that they would be returned to us at the conclusion of hostilities. We never saw the items again, nor did we ever request their return after the war.

We began to hear from our friends, neighbors, and employers that they, too, had been interviewed by the FBI about us, and that a number of "routine" questions were being raised, particularly about the actions and sentiments of my father. The chickens were coming home to roost, as they say.

My frustrations grew as, day after day, I encountered roadblocks in every direction. Before long, the frustration boiled into tangible anger at my father's stubbornness and extreme nationalism. He had, I believed, caused me embarrassment and a questioning of my own self-worth. Needless to say, my situation and feelings did nothing to create a harmonious home life for the three of us. My "move out" fund was growing too slowly, and I blamed Papa for that too—I would have access to employment if only he had secured some form of official status.

Tension in our home over national sympathies and citizenship was not new. It had been building steadily during the years leading up to and beyond America's entry into the war. Most of our family's friends, first-generation Germans or Austrians, had almost without exception obtained American citizenship soon after their arrival in this country. They were good people who had merged into their newly adopted land and its culture gracefully, but who had drifted away from us to ostensibly avoid Papa's speeches and concerts.

To the best of my memory, as Hitler rose to power in Germany, our friends were highly supportive of his early leadership, applauding his moves to bring Germany out of the morass of social upheaval and depression that had occurred in the years after the First World War. Many had relatives still living in Germany who wrote glowing accounts of the "marvelous things that were happening in the homeland." If the letter writers were to be believed, everybody had good jobs with stable incomes, miles of magnificent autobahns to drive, and a "new pride" in their country. This information was supplemented by short-wave radio propaganda designed for Germans all over the world, broadcasts in which Germany was pictured as once again taking "its rightful place in the world." Papa was a regular and avid listener, but when he tried to share those broadcasts with his friends, they were understandably disbelieving.

Papa's loyalty to Germany only grew stronger, however. Even with international conflicts rising, he enthusiastically supported the direction Hitler was taking Germany and proclaimed his approval of the new leader to anyone within hearing range.

As the Nazi movement progressed, more and more outrages of the regime were being reported in the US press, and Papa found himself beginning to stand alone among our friends in his nationalistic sentiments. Within the year, as the international press steadily revealed daily atrocities being committed by the Nazis, a number of our German-American friends began to take a different view of the happenings in their homeland, becoming less and less supportive of the Nazi movement. Any remaining loyalty they may have had for the new government rapidly faded after hard evidence was published about the Kristelnacht horror in 1938, subsequent persecution of the Jews, book burnings, destruction of dozens of synagogues throughout Germany, concentration camps, and the ultimate subversion of the courts and the Church by the Nazi hierarchy.

Despite all that, Papa remained relentless, continuing to proclaim the "wonders" that Hitler had achieved and "what he had done for the *Vaterland*." He derided our friends who questioned that direction, saying that they were nothing more than the victims of the American press, which he insisted was being manipulated by the Jews to print only the evils of Nazism.

No matter the argument to the contrary, Papa would not accept the cautions and criticisms of his closest friends to moderate his position on Hitler and his government. In fact, his pitch and volume became all the more intense. "No," he would shout out at Mutti, or at Carl and Nettel when they came to visit, if conversation even slightly skirted political issues. He declared that recently adopted, "so-called" good Americans were nothing more than hypocrites, hiding behind the shield of American citizenship so they could make a good living and turn their backs on Germany. He was not about to become an American citizen just so he could make a solid living for himself and his family, refusing to be, in his view, "two-faced about the real issues." Again and again, he shouted the words "No" and "Never," proclaiming that he was the only one true to himself and his beliefs, that he was as good an American as the rest of those "hypocrites," vowing they would soon see the error of their ways.

One night stands out in my memory during that most intense of times. I was nineteen and had never been to a formal event, so it was to be a special night for Papa, Mutti, and me. Aunt Nettel was a gifted seamstress and had sewn a vibrant peach-colored dress for Mutti. I wore my gray striped graduation suit with my good shoes, and Papa donned an outfit he kept in a plastic bag for such occasions. I secretly thought we were overdressed, but when I saw the elegant portico and interiors, I was glad Aunt Nettel had prepared us. This was not the neighborhood we lived in.

Carl and Nettel had a number of friends who also worked in minor capacities at the Czechoslovakian Embassy, where Carl was employed. Since the ambassador was away on official business, the group gave a birthday party at the embassy for a close friend and invited others to join them for the occasion. Carl and Nettel asked my parents and me as their guests. There were nearly twenty people of all ages, married and single, and mixed nationalities of German, Czech, and Austrian, almost none of whom my parents knew. Most spoke English, and I made it a point to say hello to everyone. Papa seemed to be enjoying himself and staying clear of political topics, and I was grateful to see the congenial, entertaining side of Papa we had not seen in quite some time.

Dinner was a delightful buffet, with much drinking of champagne before and after the meal. Later came singing, cigars, cigarettes, and snifters of cognac or brandy. Most everyone was feeling a bit giddy and appearing to having a fine time. The conversations continued in several small groups, sometimes spilling over and becoming a topic for everyone in the spacious and elegant room. Small talk ranged from sports to politics, along with concerns about the current tensions in Europe.

At one point, a tall, rangy young man who had been clowning around all evening—and who was by now "about three sheets to the wind"—stood up and captured the group's attention. He took out a small comb from his pocket and stroked it through his black hair, combing several strands over his forehead. He then held half the comb under his nose, gave a perfect Nazi salute, and shouted a ribald comment. The guests burst out in raucous laughter—all except for Papa. An imitation of Hitler was not a joking matter for him. He stood and roared like a bull moose in the Maine woods, proclaiming in full voice, "I refuse to be insulted by people like you! You should be ashamed to make slanderous remarks about the leader of the German nation. I refuse to be a part of this and we are leaving." With that, he grabbed Mutti by the arm, and the three of us left with everyone else either dumbstruck or tittering nervously. I remember to this day the humiliation I felt and how I wished the floor would swallow me up as we hurried out of the room, gathered our coats, and disappeared through the nearest door.

This tirade was expressive of Papa's warped and biased thinking. Anyone slightly rational could shoot his theories and beliefs to hell, but with Papa, rationality did not play a part in loyalties. Mutti, trying to be the good wife, offered little support for his views but believed fervently that it was more important to keep the peace. At least externally, she agreed that "the man of the house knows what's best and right" and that everyone else should go with the flow. I admit, I had lived with Papa long enough to know better than to argue with him about politics.

When I recall that evening, some fifty years later, I have the same sick, humiliated feeling I did that night as I followed my father out of that room. Over the years I have forgiven myself. Living with Papa, there was often nothing more I could do than follow.

The FBI's initial search of our home was not the end of the investigation into our family. The Bureau continued their probing, to the point that Mutti became greatly concerned we might be required to relocate to a city other than Washington or, more seriously, that Papa would face incarceration.

Me, I was more concerned about my ability to enter the armed forces. After the declaration of hostilities by our country, the draft went into high gear. Thousands of young men around my age were being drafted—but not me. Apparently, my status as

Enemy Alien put me into an unacceptable category and I was free to go about my life as usual. I tried for months to enlist in any one of the armed forces, but it was always the same answer: "Sorry, we can't use you just now."

In the meantime, German submarines were stationed off our east coast, regularly sinking dozens of oil tankers bound for our allies. The Merchant Marine crews manning these ships were being decimated, and the government desperately sought replacements by posting large colorful posters that appealed for patriotic volunteers. But even *they* wouldn't take me. I began to feel like a leper or pariah, uncomfortable being a civilian. I had the sense I was being diagnosed by others as "unfit for military service," categorized as 4-F, an unfit human being, or worse yet—"a goddamn draft dodger."

In May of 1942, I turned twenty-one—the age required to apply for final citizenship papers. I had made my first independent move toward becoming an American citizen three years prior, and I assumed it would only be a matter of days before I would hear from the civil court to appear for the naturalization ceremony.

The war was heating up in the Pacific. The Battle of Midway became the first major engagement in which our Navy prevailed against the overwhelming strength of the Japanese naval forces. The resounding defeat of the enemy was welcome news. This battle signaled the slow turning of the tide of the enemy's dominance in the Pacific.

I continued making efforts to enlist, visiting the recruitment offices for each branch of the US military at least once a week, and each time I was turned down. I had pretty much accepted the fact that I was going to spend the rest of the war as a civilian in Washington, but I didn't like the idea and continued to hope that my final citizenship papers would come through any day and open new doors for me.

The city was now crowded by thousands of new workers arriving from all parts of our country; workers were desperately needed in all government arenas but particularly in the War and Navy Departments. Washington's streets became flooded with uniformed personnel from every branch of US service as well as with foreign ally military officials. It was both an anxious and exciting time, but I couldn't feel part of any of it.

Shortly after New Year's Day, 1943, I met a couple of fellows at one of the bars I frequented. After we had hoisted and toasted a few, I didn't get the heady and happy effect that a few drinks normally brought me. So, I bid my friends adieu for the evening and decided to take a walk. It was about 1:00 a.m., bitter cold with a light January snow falling on an already white city.

For almost an hour, I walked without any particular destination in mind. As I emerged from my woozy doldrums, I neared the Lincoln Memorial and suddenly realized that in all the time I had lived in Washington, I had never seen this memorial at night, except in pictures. I had been here many times in daylight with hundreds of carefree tourists and schoolchildren milling about, but I had never been present for this captivating sight at 2:00 a.m.

As I approached the beautiful memorial, with its magnificent statue of Lincoln seated on the massive chair and the bright lights revealing his every facial feature, I found myself in awe. I realized I had not seen a solitary car or person for the last hour; it was quiet except for the soft sifting of light snow. Lincoln seemed to be staring directly at me with his enormous shaggy head bent slightly forward and the semblance of a smile on his face. I turned and silently reread each of the famous words inscribed upon the walls of the enclosure surrounding his statue.

> *Four score and seven years ago our fathers brought forth on this continent, a new nation, conceived in Liberty, and dedicated to the proposition that all men are created equal.*
>
> *Now we are engaged in a great civil war, testing whether that nation, or any nation so conceived and so dedicated, can long endure. We are met on a great battle-field of that war. We have come to dedicate a portion of that field, as a final resting place for those who here gave their lives that that nation might live. It is altogether fitting and proper that we should do this.*
>
> *But, in a larger sense, we cannot dedicate — we cannot consecrate — we cannot hallow — this ground. The brave men, living and dead, who struggled here, have consecrated it, far above our poor power to add or detract. The world will little note, nor long remember what we say here, but it*

can never forget what they did here. It is for us the living, rather, to be dedicated here to the unfinished work which they who fought here have thus far so nobly advanced. It is rather for us to be here dedicated to the great task remaining before us — that from these honored dead we take increased devotion to that cause for which they gave the last full measure of devotion — that we here highly resolve that these dead shall not have died in vain — that this nation, under God, shall have a new birth of freedom — and that government of the people, by the people, for the people, shall not perish from the earth.

Abraham Lincoln
November 19, 1863

I must have remained there in the silence for a full half hour. As I pivoted to leave, I glanced at my watch and saw that it was past 3:00, then looked over my shoulder for one last glimpse of the towering figure. It was a defining moment in my life that has stayed with me ever since.

As I made my way home, my head now clear, I felt deeply that whatever I had experienced was a singular event meant for me alone, and one that somehow fate had arranged. I am not a religious person, but that night moved me so profoundly that I was able to look forward to whatever lay ahead with relative calm, and with no more anger or disappointment. My new attitude was: whatever will be, will be.

Rudy Jensen

On March 13, 1943, I received the official "Greetings" from the President of the United States that millions had already received: an order that stated I was to be inducted into military service. This induction would be determined by a draft board made up of "my neighbors," and I would eventually become one of the already eight million service men and women serving their country.

I doubt very many men who received this letter were as delighted as I was, but for me, my reaction was pure jubilation. I had not yet faced the fact that Mutti and Papa did not know I had enlisted, let alone been accepted to the US military—forces that would face their beloved Germany.

nineteen

Civie to GI

Three lost days later, and in a thankfully forgotten memory of how those came to pass, I found myself at the doorstep of our Washington apartment, suffering a weighty hangover but beginning a heartfelt farewell, one that severed me from my home and my parents with a finality I had not anticipated.

Certainly, my parents' feelings were mixed. Mutti, although not happy to see her "baby boy" go off to war, expressed relief for me; she knew how I had agonized waiting for acceptance into the armed forces and the war. Papa gave me a long and strong hug and whispered in my ear, "good luck to you in what may lie ahead." I was startled; that embrace was the clearest sign of affection in what must have been years.

The war had taken its toll in our apartment. Papa and I had ceased talking about the war, or about anything for that matter, even our beloved baseball team. After my announcement, no one mentioned that I was about to fight the land of my birth, nor did we speak of our relatives in Germany whom I must now consider enemies.

On the cool and rainy morning of March 23, 1943, I left for an experience that was to be a major turning point in my life—a 27-month journey that would leave its sharply defining impact upon me. Yet despite leaving home, I was not able to leave behind the fact that I was being drafted into the American Army Air Force, not only as a German citizen, but also as an Enemy Alien.

War does strange things.

My status proved to be quite a dilemma for both the military and for me. It was obvious that the FBI investigation of our family had at least revealed that my own record was clean, with no subversive activities recorded in my personal behavior and actions. But this was not the case for my father. The Bureau continued to doggedly pursue Papa's friends from the present and past as well as his current and past employers, seeking information about his loyalties and beliefs. Since the Bureau was unable to link him with any overt acts of sedition, things were relatively quiet at home when I left. Only six months would pass, however, before Father was embroiled in another problem with the FBI, one that came very close to being a major disaster for our little family.

At the Induction Center, we received our shots, uniforms, and assignments. I was to be a member of the United States Army

Air Forces and was put aboard a troop train heading for "someplace." I learned quickly that in the wartime military, we would not be told *where* we were going, *how* we were going, or *when* we were going. Instead, troop trains traveled slowly, using circuitous routes to mystery destinations.

Near the end of our second day on the train, we noticed a distinct change in vegetation and a notable warming trend in the weather. Soon after, the train halted in a deserted area of heavy pine forest and the sergeant in charge of our car yelled out, "OK, everybody out, and in single file by the outside of the car. It's time for short arm inspection!" *Short arm?* We hadn't been issued any weapons, so what the heck arms were they going to check? We soon found out. They were checking us new inductees for signs of venereal diseases.

My "boot training" took place in Miami Beach where the Army Air Force had occupied the entire city and had taken over all hotels, beachfront properties, golf courses, and any other facility that could be used while training tens of thousands of men in the rudimentary requirements of becoming soldiers. For whatever reason, I was assigned to a large group of guys who came primarily from the Kentucky and West Virginia hills and coal mines.

I had written on my civilian jobs record that I had been an automotive parts clerk, and the Army classifications department took that literally, immediately targeting me for Air Force clerical school after boot training. Not exactly my strong suit. However, since they were not able to place me right away, I had the "pleasure" of serving *two* boot training experiences, each twelve weeks long, the second one extending through July and August. Excluding combat, due to the sultry and humid air, this was probably the most miserable time of my whole Army experience. *I asked for this?* I said to myself. I had volunteered to fight for my country, not sit behind a desk.

During the latter few weeks of my second round of boot training, I received an official-looking piece of mail. Much to my pleasure, a court date had been set for my final citizenship hearing and I was summoned to appear in the District Court in Washington. With great anticipation, I made an appointment with the top sergeant and asked to see the commanding officer of our group to request a three-day pass to attend the hearing. Long story short: "Permission Denied." Reason: I had not been in the service long enough to qualify for a three-day pass. They didn't give a damn about how important citizenship was to me and were perfectly happy to keep me in the service as an Enemy Alien. Two weeks later, I received orders for my first base assignment. Again, destination unknown.

This time our train chugged along for three days and nights, with long stops on side rails to allow other trains to pass about every two or three hours. Most station and city signs had been covered or removed and our destination was once again a big mystery. By "reading" the sun, I was able to determine that we were generally moving westward. The majority of the troops bet we were bound for "Frisco" and from there to the Pacific, assuming that was why we had trained in Miami Beach in that insufferable climate. But on the morning of the third day, we arrived in Denver, Colorado.

Looking westward from the troop train on that bright and crisp September morning, I could clearly see the magnificent peaks of the Rockies, which were already painted with an early coat of white. I was captivated. We ended up at Ft. Logan, an old former Army base located a few miles outside of Denver. Ft. Logan, now under Air Force jurisdiction, had become a training base for Air Force clerical trainees, who, after ten weeks of training, would be shipped to various air bases around the country.

I was keenly disappointed in this new assignment and felt that the tables were once again turned against me. For weeks on end, I endured this nonsense and wondered if this really was the Air Force or some secretarial finishing school, though we did continue daily physical training sessions coupled with rifle marksmanship and bayonet drill. I guessed that even clerks had to learn how to defend themselves in a pinch.

One reprieve was that the assignment was not nearly as odious as boot training had been, and the cool weather made me feel vigorous and energetic. We had a day off each week, and all of us took off for Denver, which, incidentally, was one great soldiers town. I made frequent visits to the Ship's Tavern in the Brown Palace Hotel and to Zeitze's Buckhorn Steak House near the southern area near the city's railroad tracks. These places were loaded with reminders of the characters of the early west. Among the personalities who had made Denver their home in those early years were Horace Tabor, better known as the "Silver Baron," who later built the Brown Palace Hotel with his newfound wealth and married "Molly," later better known as "The Unsinkable Molly

Brown," the heroine passenger and survivor of the *Titanic*.

But it wasn't history I was seeking on those many weekend trips to Denver. Soldiers rarely had to buy their own drinks in any of the better bars; civilians were always ready to set one up for a man in uniform who could look thirsty enough—or lonely enough. The ladies were likewise friendly and generous with their time and company.

Early in my forays into one of the Denver nightclubs, I met a little honey. We spent much time together during the following weeks, dancing, drinking, and enjoying dinners when she wasn't working. As a member of a quartet of chorus dancers, she performed twice each evening, once during the dinner hour and again for the late show. The fact that she was part of a nightclub act at the Chez Paris made our relationship even more interesting. In fact, after several weeks, it became a sort of "steady thing." She even gave me an 8x10 professional glossy photo of herself that I proudly took back to the barracks and hung on the wall over my bunk. At the bottom of the picture, she had penned an intimate message. I got the standard razzing from my fellow mates who were probably both stunned and jealous.

Our barracks had to stand for inspection each week and we were required to clean from top to bottom: no dust on ledges, everything in an exact order in footlockers, and bedding made tight enough so that a nickel thrown on the bunk bounced back up three inches. The inspection was made on Saturday mornings by a second lieutenant who was the group commanding officer, closely followed by our top sergeant with his trusty clipboard. The officers wore white gloves and used them to check for dust on ledges, windowsills, and slats under the beds. If the gloves came back with dirt, the offending soldier would be "restricted to barracks" for the weekend. If there were more than two or three offenders, the whole barracks would be put on restriction for the same period. Needless to say, the motivation for cleanliness was high. God help any poor bastards who would cause an entire barracks to lose out on a day-and-a-half leave in Denver.

There were no rules against displaying a picture of a wife or girlfriend, but absolutely no photos of pin-up girls were allowed. Any picture was to be displayed only in a designated place, just above the shelf over the coat hanger bar of the soldier's bunk. I had placed the picture of my new sweetie where it should be, but I had to admit it sure didn't look like a picture of my wife or girlfriend back home.

On inspection day, a pair of my shoes covered the bottom portion of the photo where the very personal note was written. When Lieutenant "Asshole" came to my bunk, his eyes immediately zeroed in on the picture and he snarled, "Soldier, that's a violation of regulations—you're displaying a pin-up girl. Take it down, NOW! Put this man on restriction, Sergeant."

Standing at rigid attention, looking straight forward and not at him, I responded with pleasure: "Sir, that's my girlfriend. She's a professional dancer and gave me that picture just last week. You may look at the inscription she wrote on the bottom if you wish."

The lieutenant barked at the sergeant to take the picture

down and give it to him. The sergeant obliged. Lt. "Asshole" stared at the provocative photo for a long moment, his face turning beet red as he read the inscription, clearly not one written for the casual fan of the chorus line. He muttered something unintelligible and without further comment tossed the picture onto my bed and marched stiffly down to the next set of bunks. It was all I could do to stifle a smile.

Officer hierarchy in the Army Air Force and other branches of the Army started at the lowest level with the rank of second lieutenant, the group that enlisted men often referred to as "The Ninety Day Wonders." The "Wonders" were typically selected to go to OCS (Officer Candidate School) almost immediately after being inducted into the service, usually because they had a degree or were well on the way toward finishing one at the time they were drafted. Some were allowed to finish their college work after they were inducted and then went on to OCS; others were sent to ASTP (Army Specialized Training Program) schools. They generally completed requirements to achieve their second lieutenant status in about ninety days.

My experience with the "Ninety Day Wonders" was generally negative. Many began officer training with rather limited backgrounds and did not automatically graduate from OCS as examples of superior intelligence. I was again seeing the benefits of higher education and feeling the sharp bite of being a second-class citizen. In almost every way, the life of the officer and the enlisted man were distinct; we were separated by pay, living quarters, status, respect, and privilege.

Regardless of our feelings about the hierarchy, one of the first things we learned as enlisted men was that The Articles of War demanded a strict code of conduct: commanding officers were to be obeyed without question. Failure to do so could result in a court martial charge, incarceration, or even execution in serious cases. We were commanded to respect the uniform and what it stood for, hence the required hand salute each time an enlisted man encountered an officer, or each time a junior officer met another officer of senior rank. This sound and effective system has withstood the test of time and wars through the centuries.

I had been at Ft. Logan for about a month when I requested a new date for my citizenship hearing, sending my letter directly to the department from which I had received the first notice. Weeks passed with no response to my request. I was halfway across the country now and wondered how all of this was going to shake out. *Was I going to stay in the US Air Force as an Enemy Alien until the end of the war?* I wondered.

Upon the more or less satisfactory completion of my clerical training at Ft. Logan, I was assigned with several squadrons of my fellow clerks to "someplace." Two days later, we arrived at Love Field in Dallas, Texas, where we were assigned as Permanent Party Personnel, a segment of the Air Transport Command (ATC) headquartered at this location. Love Field functioned as an aircraft supply depot; its chief mission was to ferry or transport brand-new and reconditioned combat aircraft to training bases all over the nation, and sometimes to foreign bases. All types of aircraft, including heavy and medium bombers, fighter planes, and personnel carrier aircraft were flown out. The operation required large numbers of maintenance personnel and pilots, including a significant squadron of the WAAF (Women Auxiliary Air Force). A surprising number of female pilots were utilized in this noncombatant service, and they compiled an outstanding flight and safety record.

My assignment as a Permanent Party was considered an enviable one. It could mean having a cushy job "flying a desk" in some service records department for the duration of the war, not to mention that the barracks were spacious, clean, and located conveniently to all base facilities. As permanent staff, I worked regular office hours, 8:00 to 5:00, five and a half days a week, and was issued a pass that allowed me to leave the base at all hours and return by 8:00 the next morning. This was an almost unheard-of privilege. Best of all, we had a free shuttle bus service at our disposal that took us into Dallas (about twelve miles distance) every hour on the hour, twenty-four hours a day. If Denver was a great town for soldiers, Dallas was even better. As many a soldier in the Air Force would say, "Man, you've got it made." And I did.

Even as clerks, we stood daily personal inspection and weekly barracks inspection. We also served a 24-hour stint of guard duty once per month, four hours off and four hours on. We were stationed at guard posts all around the perimeter of the massive airfield on which hundreds of new planes were parked awaiting delivery. Our standing orders were to fire at anyone who failed to stop upon command, and anyone who was unable to give the password for the day would be placed under arrest.

While stationed there, I had again applied for cadet training to become a waistgunner in the Air Force. The answer came quickly and in writing: "Sorry, applications for cadet training are not being accepted from candidates of German nationality." The perennial label had jumped up and bitten me once again. I had thought being in the Air Force might have given me a better shot than I had before I was drafted, but it wasn't to be.

During mail call one late November day, I again received an official letter announcing a court hearing for my citizenship papers, but this time the court was the US Courthouse in Denver. I was elated. Maybe this time I could make it. One of the benefits of my position was that we could often hitch a ride to any destination the dozens of planes headed each day, then return on another ATC-assigned plane. I could easily get to Denver and back to Dallas on a three-day pass, so I rushed over to the top sergeant's office to gain permission to speak to the commanding officer, a major, regarding my request. The CO was sympathetic, but not sympathetic enough to authorize my plan, as Denver was beyond the allowable distance for a three-day pass. Instead, because I had been in the service more than six months by this time, he would authorize a 7-day furlough. It might seem like an ideal solution, but it would eat into my regular furlough of ten days that I was soon to have. Without much choice, I decided to take the 7-day furlough, flying first to my hearing in Denver, then planning to hitch a ride to DC and back so that I could spend at least three or four days with my folks.

Once I made it to Denver, I rounded up a couple of my instructors from Ft. Logan who knew me and were willing to be my required witnesses. At the courthouse, I rushed through the swearing-in ceremony, became an American citizen, then dashed off to catch an ATC plane ride to DC—but I missed it. My alternative was to catch an eastbound passenger train and hope to make the best of the five days remaining on my furlough. It was probably stupid to even try, but I did make it back home to spend a day and a half with Mutti and Papa.

My parents seemed so relieved that I was being assigned to mundane clerical tasks that the atmosphere in the apartment was more relaxed than it had been for months. Papa shared no German newspapers or letters from friends overseas, and Mutti made several of my favorite dishes. She also took me aside to say she was glad for me that I got the citizenship status I so wanted. I sensed she still had mixed feelings: she had always tried to see my side of things, but her heart had rested in Friedrichshaven, her hometown in southern Germany. We never mentioned in front of Papa that his German son was now an American citizen.

After my short stay, I was on my way back to Dallas, arriving at the base only three hours before my deadline. I immediately learned that one of my clerical buddies had applied for a transfer out of the Air Transport Command and into a tactical (combat) unit. Uneasy and unwilling to spend the rest of the war in this safe haven, I followed suit.

twenty

In Position

My request for transfer to aerial combat was granted; apparently, they needed aerial gunners more than they needed desk clerks. It was nearly the end of the war and the casualties in the Eighth Air Force were already far beyond predictions. I suspected I was admitted to active combat as an Enemy Alien largely because Allied forces were running out of airmen.

I was trained once again, this time for ten intensive weeks in an Air Force gunnery school in Laredo, Texas, about two hundred and fifty miles from Dallas. Our one hundred members of Class Number 16 graduated in April, 1944, prepared for assignments to heavy bomber B-24 crews. I had finally earned the highly prized silver wings of an aerial gunner.

Being a gunner hadn't been my dream; I had wanted to become a combat pilot—and I applied for that role more times than I could count. Each time, however, the superior officer who took such requests had the same response: "You know that is an officer position." Most COs never outwardly stated the subtext—"I understand you are a German citizen"—but the times they did, I would repeat: "Yes, by birth I am German . . . but America's my country."

Their standard response was, "Oh."

"I know these are also officer positions," I'd add, "but if you ever need a navigator. . . ."

Eventually, I stopped asking. The officers charged with my supervision as a cadet could not hand over a B-24 bomber and its crew to a young man born in Hamburg and raised by a Hitler loyalist. Papa was still under surveillance of the FBI as I flew over Germany for the US Eighth Air Force, placed in a crew position as far away from the bomber's controls as possible.

From Laredo I shipped out with several dozen other newly graduated gunners to a large airbase outside Lincoln, Nebraska, where we were to be assigned to our respective bomber crews before going overseas. For two straight weeks, we never saw the sun; high winds and slashing rain pummeled the base. My job was daily KP duty, applying the high-level skills I learned in boy scout camp. Meanwhile "the Brass" were taking their time matching officers and enlisted men to make up balanced crews. As it turned out, it was worth the wait.

The day finally arrived when we all came together in an outsize hanger to meet our crews. There were four officers in each: a pilot, co-pilot, navigator, and bombardier. In addition, six enlisted men served as the engineer, radio operator, and four gunners. The pilot of the crew to which I was assigned was a serious young man of twenty-one, who would "celebrate" his twenty-second birthday during our fourth mission over Germany. When I got to know this young pilot, I could see why he would be better at the job than I would.

Our bombardier, who at thirty-six was the oldest of the crew, had just started pre-law studies when he was drafted. We called him Ball turret gunner Red, and we had a hard time keeping him sober, except when we were flying missions. Overall, we were an amalgamation of ten distinct men, married and unmarried, highly educated and not, each with a unique background. The diversity made no difference; we were going to be a team and that meant sticking together through hell or high water to meet our goals.

After we'd had a few days to get acquainted, we were moved to our next training airbase: Biggs Field, just outside of El Paso, Texas, a few miles from the dusty Mexican border town of Juarez. Here we would begin to fly together as a crew and become more proficient in the skills needed for our positions. Our planes were the early model B-24-Cs that had ten crew positions, including the ball turret and ten 50-caliber machine guns that could focus terrific firepower against attacking enemy aircraft. We flew for hours each day over the hot Texas desert, practicing maneuvers that included dropping dummy bombs on mock targets in the desert, and firing at plywood silhouette targets on the ground or on target sleeves pulled through the air by another plane. Learning to fly in close formation was tricky, and we practiced at all altitudes, flying wing tip to wing tip with dozens of other B-24s.

Working together day after day, I soon learned that our crew had a good blend of personalities, and morale ran high even though it had been only a short time since we had come together as strangers. On bomber crews, as officers and enlisted men served together to form an effective working team, rank was not an issue; only the job at hand mattered. Each of the men was a specialist in his assignments and was expected to perform at maximum effectiveness during all practice missions, and later in combat. The pilot was the unquestioned "Plane Commander"—exactly that of a ship Captain at sea—and his word was final on every aspect of the operation of the aircraft as well as of the crew's function.

Our training program as a crew moved into high gear by our second week at Biggs Field. We flew six to eight hours daily and attended ground school for additional hours in the afternoons. We flew at night as well as during the day to allow our radio operator and navigator additional time to hone their skills under varying conditions. Each day, we also had one hour of rigorous physical fitness training under the broiling Texas sun. When we had a chance to get some relaxation, four or five of us would toodle over the border and visit Mexico. It was always an adventure and usually a struggle to bring Red back through the main gate, with two of us holding him upright past the guards.

We came through our ten-week training session as a crew in good shape; all of us had become sharper in every respect, and a few days later, we flew to Topeka, Kansas, for final uniform and equipment issue. We were set to fly our plane across the Atlantic, but Red had a little problem with sobriety the night before and didn't get back to base. With an AWOL ball gunner, our crew lost out on the opportunity to fly our own plane across the sea. Instead, we had to go over on a troop ship, which took ten long days of rough and wild seas, plaguing most of us with seasickness.

The trans-Atlantic journey was further enlivened by two German submarine alerts. Lucky for Red, this was one of his first infractions and we were a collection of patient crewmates. About halfway across the ocean, the rumor mill was sparked, and all possibilities for our destination were considered—England, Italy, Africa.

Finally, our ship landed at Liverpool, England, pulling into the harbor with dozens of other crew boats. I'll never forget the British Red Cross ladies working from an old army cook wagon with grace and good humor, serving us as we hunkered down in a cold and miserable rain on the Liverpool train platform. After a meal of hot steaming tea and enormous mashed potato sandwiches (yes, England was suffering food shortages), the several hundred of us and our baggage were shunted onto an overnight train to Scotland.

Our next stop was for a 10-day combat orientation conducted on a British base in Northern Ireland. Instructors at this base brought us up to date on the latest techniques the German Luftwaffe (Air Force) were using against the thousands of allied bombers that were now streaming over cities day and night. In these latter months of 1944, the Luftwaffe had been significantly reduced in strength and number, but they were now using entirely new methods of attack in defense against our bombers and those of Britain's Royal Air Force. Despite our use of fighter planes to escort our bombers during missions, the Germans were still wreaking havoc with their attacks. The orientation sessions proved to be extremely helpful, especially to gunners, who were much better prepared to meet the enemy in the air than we would have been without the last-minute analysis.

Our American 8th Air Force was based in England and included three major bomber divisions: the first and third divisions were entirely equipped with the Boeing B-17 while our second division flew B-24 bombers. (This fostered a bit of friendly rivalry—the B-17 crews fondly referred to our B-24s as the crates the 17s came in.) Each division mustered ten to twelve groups, and each group was typically comprised of four squadrons.

In late August, 1944, our crew was bussed from Northern Ireland to a permanently assigned airbase and assigned to the 445th Bomb Group, 700th Squadron, about twenty miles from Norwich, in the southeastern quadrant of Britain near the tiny village of Tibenham. For an eighteen-year old recent high school graduate who had never been more than eighty miles from home, it was all quite an experience.

Tibenham was known for being friendly to Yanks. In fact, as our bus pulled into the base, we spotted one reason the US men were so welcome. In the midst of a severe food shortage in the village, children lined up along a wire fence while the airmen on the other side pushed rations and candy bars through the openings. There was a kind of romance between the American troops and the village families. Whatever happened to the Yanks always deeply affected the village.

Ours was but one of several hundred air bases, both British and American, scattered primarily over the southeastern and southwestern portion of England. Like the majority of these bases, ours was situated on farmland, an open rural area that had been confiscated by the British government for military use. The base had been operational for about a year before we got there and had compiled an impressive record of successful missions against the enemy.

We were immediately billeted to our quarters, a rectangular metal building that was similar to those built for the Royal Air Force. It was actually an elongated corrugated sheet metal structure, measuring about sixty feet in length and thirty feet in width, with a door at each end and eight small windows on each side. There were two pot-bellied coal-burning stoves that, if you could get enough fuel, would keep the unit fairly comfortable, except in unusually cold weather.

Five crews of enlisted men, thirty men in all, were to call this "home sweet home." Surrounded by farmland, it was not unusual to be awakened at daybreak by the lowing of the dairy cows feeding under our windows—a bucolic scene, but one that was to be replaced each day by roaring engines.

twenty-one

Kassel Changes Everything

Tibenham, England

September 27, 1944

Since 1944, my life has been divided into two parts: Before Kassel and After Kassel. Before Kassel, the question was: Will we see Christmas in the States this year? After Kassel, the question was: Will we ever see Christmas again?

In beginning to write this life story, I never considered starting anywhere other than at that day in September when thirty-five planes and their crews left our base and disappeared from our lives. This is the rest of that story.

Our crew was just settling into the Tibenham base that was to be our home for months, perhaps years, depending upon how long this war lasted. We were told that we were part of a historical assault: the last attack on Hitler's forces. Stopping his aerial forces here could mean stopping them everywhere.

Our crew was listed to fly in a large-scale mission the next day, but at about 6:00 that evening, an officer rounded us up to tell us we had been scrubbed from the next day's roster. As new flyers, he explained, we first needed to participate in a night orientation exercise to acquaint us with the targeted field and surrounding areas under blackout conditions. Another crew from our own barracks was assigned to the mission in our place, and my mates and I headed to the airplane hangars to meet our instructors for the night-flying lessons. We didn't even try to hide our keen disappointment over not being able to make the next day's mission. We needed to fly thirty-five missions before we could return home, and as of now we were at zero.

We slept in that next morning, having not returned to our sacks after training until well after midnight. I remember the comforting drone of hundreds of bombers circling while forming in the skies above ours and neighboring bases, thinking, *We were supposed to be in that formation.*

Later that day, security was released and word spread around the base that the mission this day was Kassel, Germany. It was a critical hub in the heart of highly industrialized Ruhr Valley, which contributed mightily to the production of German war materials. This city had been a target several times in past months, but none of the raids had been successful enough to close down the war factories completely. Today's raid was expected to finish off their production center for good. Pretty routine, but not quite.

It was customary on the American bases in England to welcome home the flyers of the day, waving arms and screaming congratulations. But today when we searched the sky for returning planes, we saw nothing. I noticed an unusually large group of "Big Brass" standing at the upper rails and anxiously looking through their binoculars toward the southwest—the direction of Kassel.

Far from the distance of the runway, we saw only two of our B-24s approaching the field, not in the normal pattern for landing but straight in. Crippled engines groaned distress, with wheels down and shooting off red flares indicating wounded men aboard. One plane limped along on two engines, and the other had a large piece of the vertical rudder completely torn off, also with red flares signaling that severely wounded men were aboard. Crash trucks and ambulances roared past us toward the end of the runway.

A long five or ten minutes elapsed before the third plane came hobbling in on three engines, with red flares arcing out of its fuselage. It was coming in too low; when it struck the surface it began sliding off the edge of the runway, halfway down the intended course. Normal landing procedure from routine mission returns called for the big planes to peel off the approach pattern at approximate one-minute intervals, landing quickly to clear the path for other returning crafts. Today, however, no planes followed the leaders. Another full ten minutes ticked by. Only one more of our planes emerged, both flying and landing normally. That was it. No other planes, no other men.

The reality of this loss was starkly driven home when our crew entered the mess hall for dinner that night: the two dozen surviving crew members sat spread out where 200 places were set. The usually boisterous hall was silent, solemn. Word spread that Jimmy Stewart, the Hollywood star and Army Air Force officer, had been doing some of the debriefing interviews with survivors, and that he was struggling to hold back tears.

Like the other crews, my mates and I could not eat anything. We left our plates untouched and hesitantly returned to our barracks, steeling ourselves to at least eighteen empty bunks. But not even those were present. Every trace of our friends was gone—not only the blankets and comforters, but the posters, pictures from home, weathered cribbage boards, and decks of cards. All signs of stolen moments of pure fun we had each shared with the young men were now removed, as if they had ever been here. And I had been so sure they were the lucky ones.

Citing security reasons, the results of the official, detailed investigation of the mission were not released to non-officers—and certainly not to the press and public—until long after hostilities of the war ended. We were told that to release the accounts of this day would be bad for morale and could cripple endeavors at every base.

The magnitude and impact of the disaster was multifold. It was eventually revealed that this was the highest single group loss during an air battle in the history of the entire air war conducted by the Army 8th Air Force. At that point, I began to wonder if we were ever going to see twenty missions, much less thirty-five. I also began to wonder about the wisdom of ever again arguing with fate and what it offered us at any given moment. It sounds trite perhaps to say my life changed that day, but I assure you that it did.

We learned over time that, startlingly, all the carnage occurred in about five minutes of aerial combat. From what I have since been able to piece together from my readings—primarily Eric Ratcliffe's *The Kassel Raid*—the cause of the Kassel disaster was human error. The group navigator had plotted an incorrect heading prior to reaching the primary target. This error caused the entire 445th Bomb Group to leave the protection of the Allies fighter stream, the protective shield of planes that constantly patrolled over and under the fleet of allied bombers to ward off any attack by Luftwaffe fighter planes. This procedure was called "riding shotgun" as protection for the bombers, and by that point was standard practice.

As a consequence of the navigation error, the entire group of planes from Tibenham (four had aborted and returned to base earlier) veered away from the main path to the target and were out alone like sitting ducks. The lurking German fighter pilots did not lose a moment in exploiting the grievous error made by their enemy. Some 100 enemy fighters (some accounts say up to 150) came barreling through the Air Force group, in wave after wave, firing their 20-millimeter cannon and machine guns continuously. With each passing sweep, another four or five bombers either blew up instantaneously or began a slow, deadly spiral toward the ground below. Parachutes fell through the burning debris that spilled from the sky, while red-orange blossoms of exploding aircraft marked another tomb for the nine men inside. German fighter planes, ME109s and FW190s, made up the bulk of the attacking force, and they too paid a heavy price for this slaughter. They lost 29 planes and 117 men in the air, and at least another eight men were killed after being captured.

Kassel was no doubt a sharp and painful blow to our entire crew. Having missed that mission by the narrowest of margins, the message was loud and clear that nothing during the balance of our tour could be taken for granted. Our crew was now brutally sensitized to the fact that our tour of duty was going to be a day to-day crapshoot, and that the rest of our missions would not be a series of "milk runs" as we had so naively presumed.

It was an accurate forecast.

Rumors made their way around the base that Tibenham would be closed down after such a loss. Instead, we began to see replacement planes taxi in. The next day, more than ninety of us climbed into ten serviceable aircraft and flew back to complete the mission that had claimed the lives of our friends and colleagues.

For three straight days, my crew flew nonstop missions. I barely closed my eyes, seeing those red flares again and again. Then, on the day designated as our crew rest and recuperation day, another crew manned our plane. During that run, the plane and the entire crew were destroyed in a crash over Germany.

All I could think was: *What have I done? My crew mates were drafted for this war. Why had I volunteered for it? Why couldn't I have been satisfied with the desk job in Texas?*

Maybe Papa was right.

twenty-two

—

My Mission

Tibenham, England

January 16, 1945

None of our missions were "typical," as the requirements for all participating crews varied with the length and depth to the target and the kind of enemy resistance we faced each time. Apart from Kassel, this particular one stands out in my memory.

Most combat missions over Germany had squadrons consisting of ten to twelve planes, and each group could number forty to forty-eight aircraft. Numbers of available planes varied from day to day depending on how many planes were airworthy at the time, or how many were missing in action from the day before and in process of being replaced. These numbers seemed meaningless until crews from multiple groups became airborne and began the process of "forming up" to go against the enemy. It was then that hundreds of bright silver four-engine bombers, some still in their old camouflaged paint coatings, scattered over the English skies as far as the eye could see. Within thirty or forty minutes, they began to look like huge flocks of geese. Each flock fell in behind a leader in separate and staggered Vs, heading southeast toward the European continent. I can still visualize those vast formations. To this day it reminds me of how historians describe Pickett's last charge at Gettysburg:

With battle pennants fluttering, thousands upon thousands of men, rank upon rank moved resolutely forward into a hail of withering enemy fire.

Sometimes all six crews in our barracks would fly on a given mission, but most often only two or three would be sent. The night before each mission, we were put on "alert status" and our names were listed for the next day's mission. Listed crews got to their bunks early that night and prepared for an early-morning call to rise and shine. The first hint of awakenings for me came when I heard the crunch of gravel under the wheels of the officer's jeep as he pulled up outside our barracks. He would come in shining his flashlight on a clipboard to make sure he awakened only those men who were scheduled for that day's mission. The time was generally 2:30 to 3:00 a.m. but would vary depending on the projected length of flying time to the target. That variance gave us some hint of how far we would be flying that day.

Mumbling and groaning, we would quickly dress in long johns, woolen uniforms, and two pairs of socks and sweaters. We hurried outside to our bikes to make the half-mile trip to the mess hall for breakfast, which on mission days was usually *real* eggs and ham.

From breakfast we traveled to the equipment building. Here we dressed in flying clothes to give us some protection from airborne temperatures that could exceed minus thirty to fifty degrees Fahrenheit, at altitudes of 22,000 to 28,000 feet. We each had our own lockers that contained our necessities—electric flying suits; felt booties that were also wired and plugged into the flying suit; and outerwear, which consisted of sheepskin-lined leather jackets and pants that covered the electric flying suit, white silk gloves that went under the electric corded gloves, and leather gloves. Next, we donned the all-important "Mae West" (a deflated life vest in case of water crashes), and a parachute harness that buckled around the thighs, waist, and shoulders. In the parachute room, we attached chest-type parachutes that were repackaged after every mission, by specialists to whom we would owe our lives if an emergency arose and the chutes were needed.

After dressing, each crew member went to a briefing area designated by his respective position; pilots and co-pilots, navigators, bombardiers, radio operators and engineers, and gunners filed into their respective briefings. By far, the largest group was the gunners because there were three of us on each bomber.

A curtain hung in front of a wall-sized map of Germany. It wasn't until the briefing officer pulled it aside that the target was revealed to us. Depending on the target and the depth of the indicated penetration shown by the ribbon stretched across the map, there were usually audible groans and moans. The most grumbling came when major targets like Berlin, Hamburg, Schweinfurt, or anywhere in the Ruhr Valley (known by one and all as FLAK Valley) were revealed. After briefing, we were under stern orders not to discuss with anyone any aspect of what we had seen or been told about the target until we became airborne.

From here it was out to the hardstands where our planes were parked. We piled into hulking tarp-covered six-by-six trucks that took us across the field, three crews at a time, and dropped each crew at its plane. This was the only time we could share a few laughs and jokes with our ground crew, who had been up all night prepping and fine-tuning the plane, loading gas, ammunition, and bombs. These were the unsung heroes of the Air Force and we valued them highly. They knew their plane intimately; they took pride and had a special place in their hearts for the aircraft they serviced each night. When it didn't return from a mission, they grieved mightily for the men as well as for their plane. Usually within a day after such a loss, the ground crew were assigned a replacement plane and a new flying crew.

Once all last-minute checks and adjustments had been made, thirty-five or forty heavily loaded B-24s trundled slowly out toward the take-off line, much like a chain of elephants in a circus parade, trunk to tail. Brakes constantly squealed as the planes attempted to keep position in the slow-moving line. Each carried a load of 2,800 gallons of high-test gas, at least a half ton of .50-caliber ammunition, and depending on the target, five to seven tons of bombs. The ground crew chief and his helpers would wipe their hands of grease and oil, take another swig of coffee, and make their way to their barracks for some well-deserved sack time.

The rumbling increased steadily as all planes began their series of last-minute checks, starting their engines until all four were in full voice with bright orange tongues of flame shooting out from the exhausts. Although it was generally dark, all eyes would be on the control tower, waiting anxiously for the "GO" signal of a high arcing green flare. At that signal, the first plane in line began to roll down the 6,000-foot runway.

Every once in a while, the whole mission would be "scrubbed" at this point because the weather had deteriorated unexpectedly. We remained in suspense if the flare we'd see would be green or red. On those mornings when we were at a "stand down" instead of flying, we did in reverse order everything we had done to get ready for flight, right down to crawling back in the sack around 6:30 a.m. for a couple hours of extra snooze time.

But today it was a green flare: the mission was GO. After a collective holding of breath by the crew, our heavily laden bomber inched off the runway and whooshed past the steeple of the tiny church that was the place of worship for the parishioners of Tibenham. It was always a welcome sight to pass that steeple by a couple hundred feet because that meant we had made a clean liftoff. Every thirty seconds, another bomber would roar into the darkness until all were airborne. Only then would the earlier thundering on the field give way to a steady drone from hundreds of planes circling above in the gray of an early dawn.

After an hour or so, these "Big Assed Birds" (a term of endearment by the B-24 crews) began to look more like flocks of geese, winging together and becoming one huge flock of hundreds, aiming to bring destruction to industries that were at the heart of the enemy's capacity to make war.

As we reached the English Channel, daylight spread up from the eastern horizon and allowed our visibility to stretch for hundreds of miles. The pilot and co-pilot began a series of checks while we hovered over the middle of the Channel at about 12,000 feet. After the pilot ensured the intercoms were operational and connected the cockpit voices to each crewman, the co-pilot ordered a test firing of guns from all positions: the big plane vibrated and shook violently as each gun position let loose a couple short bursts into the sea below. We were ready.

Our engineer crawled onto the catwalk in the bomb bay and began pulling the safety wires from the ten 500-lb. bombs we were carrying.

"Bombs armed and ready," his voice boomed across the intercom for all the crew to hear.

Our mission this day was a long one, deep into the southeastern part of Germany and predicted as a nine-and-a-half-hour flight, one of the longest missions we were to fly. Target: the Junkers aero engine plant located in the suburbs of Magdeberg. This plant manufactured and assembled the high-performance engines for a key twin-engine fighter aircraft in the Luftwaffe's many fighter groups. During our early-morning briefing, intelligence had revealed heavy pockets of FLAK at certain points along the way and the likelihood of Luftwaffe attacks. Our commanders had attempted to route us around the dangers as much as possible, but weather was deteriorating rapidly as we approached the target.

An undercast had begun to form below us, blocking out the view of the ground beneath our formations. There were about four or five hundred planes involved in this raid, and our group was toward the forward portion of the attacking force. The German FLAK gunners were throwing up a steady stream of cannon fire, but most of it was far below our altitude. As we neared the target, however, we suddenly saw several exploding bombers; the harrowing sight of those large orange-red blossoms meant immediate death for the crews in those planes—planes that had been right ahead of our group's formation.

Just as suddenly, we saw the reason.

The Luftwaffe had begun an attack on the forward echelon of our bomber stream and could be seen barreling through the forward elements of the formation. Although we had not seen the enemy before, we now saw the telltale evidence: dozens of small white puffs from their 20-millimeter cannon fire. We were able to spot the Luftwaffe fighter planes coming head on and barrel-rolling through the formation below and to the right of our group. As they passed well below, we could see the leading edges of their wings ablaze from the murderous fire of machine guns and cannons they were pouring into the formations ahead of them.

All this happened in less than two minutes. Because of distance, there was no chance for us to fire at the enemy planes from our formation; all we could do was watch helplessly as they continued through those behind us, leaving burning and exploding B-24s along with others sliding steeply out of the formation, trailing heavy black smoke in their wake. Within minutes, our own P-51 fighter planes swooped in from another direction, slashing and firing into the German fighters and driving them away from the bomber stream.

As we approached the initial point of our mission, the pilot announced that we were entering the "bomb run." The pilot and bombardier were in direct communication as the pilot prepared to put the plane into its automatic pilot mode. "It's all yours," he called out. The bombardier took full control, able to control the plane's every move by the turn of dials on his Norden bomb sight. The bomb bay doors opened, sending a thunderous cold rush of air through the waist of the plane. Four plumes of white smoke erupted from the marker bombs of the bay of the lead ship—the signal for the rest of the group to do the same. The instant those bombs fell from the lead ship, our bombs and those of the forty other planes in our group dropped from their racks. Our plane lunged upward three or four hundred feet, responding immediately to its lightened cargo after releasing 5,000 pounds of bombs.

In the next twenty minutes, hundreds of our planes continually flew over the target and bombed in the same manner. This technique, developed in the latter part of the air war over Germany by the US Army Air Force, was termed "carpet bombing" or "saturation bombing" and was considered to be most effective in leveling the ground around the target within a two-mile radius.

The bomb bay doors closed and the entire formation swung sharply to the right to begin the first leg of a long journey home.

We continued to be alert to the possibility of a new attack by the Luftwaffe, but as we scanned the airspace, we could see only our own "little friends" (Allied Mustang P-51s) flying high above us—those who had been responsible for driving off the earlier attack of German fighters. They were a wonderful sight, but just as we were relaxing from the threat of another fighter attack, the sky around us once again filled with ugly black mushrooms of exploding FLAK. The bursts were uncomfortably close and were now virtually at our exact altitude in the area toward which we were flying.

Our co-pilot jumped on the intercom to get reports of damage to the plane from all positions of the crew. Fortunately, no crew member had been hit by the blasts, but a number of hits to the plane were reported, including one basketball-size hole on the left (my side), only a foot above my head. Our engineer reported that the left bomb bay door had been partially ripped away and was flapping noisily against the plane. He was instructed by the pilot to chop it free with the emergency ax. We were less than comforted by the sounds of the damaged bomb bay door as it tore loose and slammed into the underside of the fuselage before it flew off into space.

We were still at least two and a half hours deep into enemy territory before all the groups would be clear of Germany. Our greatest concern now was to keep up with the rest of the formation and not become a straggler, which the German fighters always zeroed in on. Aircraft flying with less than four engines were prime targets for the Luftwaffe. Our own fighter patrols were still well above us and readily available to pounce on the enemy if the German pilots were bold enough to push an attack against the cripples.

As we scanned the hostile skies, we noticed that our plane had begun to slip behind the forward flights, and we were now merging with a second unit that was behind us.

Pre-mission pilot training in the B-24—or in any four-engine plane—had included much practice flying time on either two or three engines. But with only half of our bomb bay doors closed, the gap caused additional drag on the plane and presented a unique challenge for our pilots. They had to manipulate and constantly readjust the throttle controls to compensate for the drag as well as for the lost engine, while at the same time not overloading the remaining three engines by demanding too much power from them.

Crawling along for what seemed to be an eternity, we continued to lose speed and altitude. As we neared the Dutch coast, we had descended to about 14,000 feet and were about to lose contact with the rest of the formations as we crossed the coastline leading to the Channel. The pilot advised the crew that the second damaged engine had begun to overheat and was causing a light trail of blue smoke to streak behind us. We proceeded over the Channel with two of our fighters riding shotgun. Our "little friends" flying above us tuned into the predicament we faced and soon were dropping toward us to form a protective cordon, one on each side, about a mile or so out.

Our pilot's voice crackled over the intercom, commanding the crew to jettison anything that would lighten the load, including guns, full ammunition boxes, flak vests, and helmets—anything that wasn't bolted down. If we had any remorse about heaving our "shooting irons" and ammo overboard, it didn't slow us down one bit. We discarded (as later estimated) over a thousand pounds out the rear escape hatch in less than five minutes. As a result, the plane responded better, though the overheating engine was still acting up and we were down to only 7,000 feet over the checkerboard plowed fields of England.

As our fear of having to bail out over the Channel or make a "ditch" landing in the water increased, those beautiful White Cliffs of Dover came into view. (We decided the writer of that song had no idea *how* beautiful they really were.) As we approached them, we were elated and relieved when the wings cleared. It was then that all of us felt we would make it.

The crippled engine was smoking heavily now as we came straight in, lining up with the main runway of our base. We hit the ground with a jarring thud and a loud squeal of burning rubber, finally rolling to a stop. A rousing cheer went up from our crew as we celebrated the completion of our 23rd mission. Only twelve more to go.

Through the years, many friends with whom I have shared "war stories" have asked how I felt about bombing my country of birth. At the time of the war, I knew none of my German relatives, with the exception of the dim memory of dear Frau Kowenhagen and her daughter, Herta, in Hamburg. I must confess I never gave that more of a thought than the general feeling of compassion I had for all the German citizens upon whom our bombs rained death and destruction. I felt sorrow for all the lives our missions may have ended. My personal anger and motivation for fighting in the war was directed toward the leaders and government of Germany for the terrible deeds they were committing in the name of their country and my land of birth. I considered that "they" were all my enemy and I was theirs. It couldn't have been any other way.

I flew my last mission on March 30, 1945, but it was one more month before I boarded a troop ship to return to the States. The ship was filled with men, most of them US infantry who had been POWs and newly released from German prison camps. There were about fifty Air Force personnel aboard; the rest were all former soldiers from various Army divisions in Europe. Some of these men had been imprisoned for as long as two years and were in a deplorable state of health. Even eating a portion of regular meals caused them to become ill; their systems were simply not accustomed to good, solid food. They looked more like scarecrows than men, and in later years when I saw some of the pictures for the first time of the concentration camp victims, these servicemen appeared similar—literally skin and bones—but all or nearly all glad to be alive.

Those of us who had suffered little of the severe physical hardship these men had endured gladly pitched in to bring food and drink to those unable to come to the ship's mess hall. It certainly made me feel thankful that I had had the good fortune to end up in the Air Force, and lucky enough not to have been forced to bail out of a crippled plane only to end up in a Nazi prison camp.

Yes, indeed, I was very thankful.

Victory in Europe Day (VE Day) had been declared on the 7th of May, 1945, while I was still on the ship in the middle of the Atlantic. The few remaining leaders of the German people were forced to sign the terms of the "Unconditional Surrender" that they had so desperately wanted to avoid. Hitler was dead, and the leading Nazis would now face a World Court comprised of members of the major Allied Forces.

Japan became the next nation to feel the wrath of the free world and would also be forced to sign terms of an "Unconditional Surrender"—but only after their people had suffered the hell and devastation of the atomic bombs dropped on Hiroshima and Nagasaki.

World War II had now officially ended, and the years 1939 to 1945 would become another vivid scar in the recorded history of the world.

twenty-three

GI to Civie

1945

I had finished my thirty-five missions, but not yet my service time, so I was happy to get a 30-day leave to return home and have the opportunity to rest and recuperate.

I don't know why it surprised me, but I felt a mix of excitement and apprehension as I approached the apartment door. Papa, who had had a trying experience of his own during my absence, was subdued and thoughtful. I'm sure he was glad to see me safe and sound, but he seemed to be stressed and was careful to avoid any conversation about the war. Mutti, on the other hand, was ecstatic that her "boy" was home again. She even attended several extra Masses to thank her God for the blessing he had bestowed on her and her family.

It wasn't easy avoiding talk of the war—my life had been consumed with it, and it was the topic all the visiting friends wanted to know about. For Papa's sake, I did a lot of changing the subject. I thanked heaven for baseball teams; their games made up the bulk of our dialogue.

Eventually, Mutti took me aside one day when Papa was at work. She had something of great importance to share with me and swore me to confidentiality. I promised never to tell Papa as we sat opposite each other, her face awash with seriousness.

It turns out that after I had been in the Air Force for about nine months, things became ever more complicated in the investigation of my father. According to Mutti, Papa had finally begun to tone down some of his strident rhetoric and expressions of nationalistic zeal. It was, however, too little too late. By this time a new development in the investigation created another crisis in our home. For the first time since the investigations had begun, Papa was called in to meet a ranking officer of the Bureau, and to face charges for deportation.

Apparently, the FBI had found something they could officially charge Papa with. During the Depression, he had made an illegal entry into the United States, when he returned from Canada after working five months at Quebec's Hotel Chateau Frontelac. Canada had always been our friendly northern neighbor and only asked of those entering from the US if they were a citizen of the United States, never actually demanding proof of such citizenship. When one returned to the States, the US customs officers asked the same question. My father obviously had answered "Yes" in order to come back in. The Bureau concluded that he had lied and would be held accountable. Though it seemed a bit of a technicality, I guessed that Papa had over the years accumulated quite a file documenting his marginal activities and spreading of propaganda. This illegal entry was likely the last straw, and with me not home to help his defense, the Bureau charged him with cause and he faced the possibility of arrest or deportation.

Poor Mutti was desperate and thrown back onto her own resources. Without a hint of her intention to either Nettel or Carl—and certainly not to Papa—she made an arrangement, but not with an attorney. Taking a day off from work, she met for an appointment she had secured with J. Edgar Hoover's personal secretary. She could not get in to see "The Boss" himself, but apparently his secretary had discussed the matter with J. Edgar after mother's phone call. When she arrived at the imposing FBI offices, my father's thick case file was sitting on the secretary's desk. Mutti pled her case and, to make a longer story short, that was the last she or anyone else ever heard of an investigation of Carl Jensen.

We will never know just how Papa's situation was resolved and what might have happened before or after Mutti's visit, but I think it proves the old adage that "it's well to know the right people in high places." J. Edgar was a frequent guest at hotel dining rooms, and my father was always his favorite and requested waiter. There was apparently something Hoover liked about Papa. For years, I've pondered their friendship. How does a German-speaking Enemy Alien become so close to our nation's chief of security? A friend once speculated that even the FBI respected the role I was playing in the war, and that may have influenced a more favorable view of the Jensen family.

As Mutti told me her "very secret" story, my mouth hung open in astonishment. Mutti was a indeed a champion. I kept my promise of confidentiality until both of my parents passed away.

I spent much of my leave calling on friends and frequenting my favorite hangouts. One of my closest bartender buddies, Ozzie Rosetti, kept me talking for the better part of one evening. By the end of our chat, he insisted that I take his little 1936 Ford the next day to go visit one of my girlfriends who lived in Maryland, a short distance from DC. He said he rarely drove the car anyway since gas was hard to get, and he was easily able to walk to his job at the restaurant.

Using my extra gas ration coupons, it was wonderful to feel independent and behind the wheel of a car again. I was cruising through the residential suburbs of Washington, looking ahead to a fine day, when I was suddenly struck broadside by a large, fast-moving car that had failed to stop at a traffic sign. The force of the impact drove me and Ozzie's car through the air into someone's front yard. The poor little car landed upside down and damaged, but I somehow emerged with only minor injuries. Here I was, home from the brutal war with not a scratch on my hide from air missions, and I get clipped in a car crash.

The driver of the other vehicle was a Navy captain and was held fully responsible. Ozzie's car was totaled. Shortly thereafter, the insurance company paid him its full market value, but so what? He couldn't, nor could anyone else, buy a new or even used car in mid-1945, as all the factories were busy producing war materials. I felt terrible giving him the bad news, but like the good guy he had always been, he shrugged it off and said, "Hell, Rudy, havva anutter bierey, you no getta hurt, thatza de main ting."

Bless that great old guy's heart. He died a only few months later. Sadly, being back on military assignment, I wasn't able to attend his funeral. He had been a bachelor all his life, but he had many caring friends among his regular customers because of his warm and affable ways. Several dozen of them attended the funeral, including Papa.

After I returned to my base in North Carolina, I had time to reflect on my visit with my parents. I was startled at the change I had perceived in my father's general demeanor. He had avoided any discourse on the recent defeat of the Nazi regime in Germany. Much later, I learned from Mutti that he was stunned by what was revealed in the news reports regarding the horrors that had been committed in the concentration camps. There was no way he could refute the evidence of the atrocities perpetrated by the German government under the rule of the Nazis.

I also learned that both my parents, along with Uncle Carl and Aunt Nettel, spent hundreds of dollars and gave extensive time and effort to purchase and box packages of emergency food and clothing to send to their German relatives. Mutti's and Nettel's family resided in Friedrichshafen, and the majority of Carl's relatives lived in Dresden. As East Germans, the Dresden relatives faced the additional burden of living under the rule of the Russians. Apparently, there were no surviving family members in Hamburg they were able to contact. So, each week for the next three years, my parents, Uncle Carl, and Aunt Nettel set up a virtual assembly line in our apartment, putting together three to four large boxes for immediate shipping.

I was now marking time at Fort Bragg, a large Air Force Rest and Recovery (R&R) facility in Greensboro, North Carolina, spending the rest of my days with Uncle Sam in relative ease and pleasure. At last, the Air Force found a way to use my German-language skills, by making me a supervisor of German POWs assigned to manicure the officer's golf course. Better yet, the Air Force had arranged a priority system for discharges based on the numerical value of points an individual soldier had earned. I had compiled a sufficient number of bonus points toward early discharge due to the number of battle decorations I was awarded during my service period. I had not been aware of this advantage, so it was an unexpected and pleasant surprise when my name moved toward the top of the long lists of GIs awaiting discharge. Ultimately, I was among the first soldiers to be discharged when the war with Japan ended in August.

I came home as a civilian in early September, 1945, and attempted to resume a normal life as quickly as possible. I admit it wasn't easy. I immediately became restless and uneasy, sleeping fitfully and drinking too much, and replaying some of the worst moments of combat. In returning to my old job at the Buick agency, I fell into a routine of nothingness. My "grand plan" had been put on hold, and I realized I was facing a fear of moving forward, of doing something important like going back to school.

And, thanks to the new GI (Government Issue) Bill, I was running out of excuses.

The GI Bill was probably the most positive thing that came out of the war for US servicemen and women—a significant and appreciated reward from a grateful government. It provided veterans with the opportunity to resume their interrupted educations, or to begin new directions through higher education or by developing skills in a chosen trade. It was a great opportunity for each and every one of us; it could mean four free years at a college pretty much of one's own choosing, with all tuition and book fees paid, and a stipend of $60 per month.

Even though I had a clear understanding of the opportunity, I still held back, and I wasn't sure why. In the military, I had been made keenly aware of how important it was to gain a higher level of education, regardless of which course of study one pursued. In fact, I had given this matter much thought before being discharged, and it occurred to me that liberal studies would be an ideal path to follow, at least during my first year of college.

Still, however, I delayed. Was it fear that I couldn't cut it if I went to college? Wasn't I confident that I could survive the demands a university would place on my scholarship or my perseverance? What had happened to that old fire in my gut, the fire that had goaded me whenever I saw privileges extended to those who were well educated? Hadn't my own lack of a degree often rankled me during my military experiences?

In the end, I can say with certainty that I would not have pursued a college degree had it not been for the GI Bill. In the absence of that, I likely would have gone into a trade school for additional honing of earlier learned skills to become a tool and die maker in industry. The Bill helped me overcome the barriers of low income and of weak scholarly inclination. After long bouts of soul searching, I finally convinced myself that regardless of my trepidation, I should follow my heart toward my earlier goals, so I began exploring college options while working at Buick with a nice advance in pay.

Just around the corner from work was Pete's Spaghetti House, the neighborhood's favorite tavern. Pete owned and operated the business and offered great Italian dinners along with a cozy bar. I used to go there for a short beer or two after work and sometimes stayed for dinner while planning the night's activities. Papa and a few of his cronies would occasionally meet me there if they had worked the day shift at the hotel. I was usually still dressed in work clothes and my old leather-flying jacket that I had brought home as a souvenir from the Air Force.

One night while Papa, a friend of his, and I were at the restaurant bar, the first heavy snowfall of the season in Washington left traffic stalled and jammed; even the streetcars bogged down. Since cabs were almost impossible to find, most homeward-bound workers were having to slog it out on foot. I noticed an attractive young lady, smartly attired in the navy-blue great coat of a WAVE (Women Accepted for Volunteer Emergency service), bustling through the doors of the restaurant. She brushed off the heavy wet flakes of snow from her uniform and cap, then removed her coat and seated herself at one of the two booths still available. I could see by the stripes on her sleeve that she held a substantial rating in the Navy. I nudged Papa and winked, nodding my head in her direction and making some comment about how lucky the Washingtonians were to have such lovely creatures serving the cause of liberty and freedom. Papa looked over and had no choice but to agree.

The restaurant was now nearly filled, with few seats available for hungry patrons, and my appetite suddenly ratcheted up considerably. I told my father and his friend that I felt I should join the lovely WAVE and share war stories. His friend poked Papa in the arm and chuckled, making a remark about the young always looking out for themselves. Papa just smiled and shook his head as I made my way over to her, where I complained about the crowded conditions and asked if she would mind sharing her booth with me.

Her steady, blue-gray eyes gazed up at me, and a small knowing smile flitted across her lips. "Sure, not at all," she murmured.

I learned that her name was Bettie Mae Brittain and that she had served in the Navy Department in Washington for the past two and a half years. Her earlier studies at a Philadelphia business school had equipped her well in the skills of shorthand, dictation, and speed typing. Starting out in the Navy's stenographer pool after Boot Camp, she rapidly advanced into an assignment at the headquarters of Admiral King, then chief of staff for the entire US naval operation during the war. She had been in that office for the past two years and had the ratings to prove it.

Over spaghetti and wine, Bettie told me she had left home at the age of seventeen and married a high-flying and popular musician from a neighboring town who was sixteen years her senior. The marriage lasted less than a year and was dissolved by mutual consent when he was drafted into the Navy. Bettie recalled that it was her heavy-handed father who made life difficult for her and her younger sister Joan in their teenage years. She felt his governance had been tyrannical and was the primary motivation for her leaving home so soon, and for rushing headlong into a marriage to an attractive older man.

I also learned that Bettie had already made plans to attend the University of Missouri at Columbia to begin studies in journalism that coming February. Her work at the Navy Department and the three months she had spent as a "gofer" for the *Washington Post* had secured her acceptance at the university.

We began dating steadily that very night.

Bettie constantly urged me onward in my own college plans, encouraging me to pursue the application process and make my commitment. Since I could pretty much have my choice of colleges as a GI, I chose my school not for its position as a viable and respected member of academia, but rather because it was located in Denver, the city I had loved since my Air Force days at Fort Logan.

Denver University was formerly the Iliff School of Theology and had become a public institution only several years earlier. Without a clear vision or goals in my mind—only a half-baked notion that I wanted to become a writer—I figured just about any good liberal arts college would do. As luck would have it, after I had been in school for almost a year, I found that Denver U.

sported a high academic rating among all Western colleges and universities of similar size. Quite by fortuitous accident, I had chosen a winner!

Bettie and I had agreed to separate, each of us going to our own schools, she to Missouri and me to Denver. We agreed (quite sensibly) that being apart for almost five months might be a good test of our feelings for each other. After that period, we could review the situation and take it from there.

Since her semester began in February and mine didn't start until March, I took her to the Union Train Station in Washington to see her off. Although it was sad and traumatic to say goodbye, I knew that our separation wasn't going to be for five months because I had a secret plan.

I had been able to work a deal to buy a sharp 1939 Packard Coupe, a top-quality car in its day. Through the help of some of my buddies at the Buick shop and different parts departments from around town, I was able to get critical parts that the former owner had not been able to secure. In fact, he'd had to put the car up on blocks for the last two years of the war, and his dilemma brought the price within my reach.

While overseas, I had been an avid gambler, squandering my pay pretty much each month. I had no wife, no need to save, and not much common sense. And sure as hell, I had no assurance that I was ever going to get out of the war alive, so I went for broke almost every month. The nice thing about the Army is that it does take care of you: free room and board, transportation to and from work, nice uniforms, and free dental and medical care. Why worry?

With an attitude like that, how could I come up short in gambling?

After losing a long series of games in the barracks and donating a lot of pay to my fellow soldiers, I had gotten into a crap game one night in January right after payday, with *big* money involved. I ended the evening with several hundred English one-pound notes (one pound equaled approximately $4) and hundreds of ten-shilling notes, valued at $2, stuffed into every pocket, inside my shirt, and even in my socks. After everyone else was broke, I made off to my bunk for a financial review to find that my net total for the evening was $2,200! The next morning, I probably did the only smart thing I ever did while overseas: I went to the base post office and sent a $2,000 money order home for safekeeping.

And so, back in DC, with a honey in St. Louis to visit, I was able to buy that Packard for $1,100 cash, plus a few extra bucks to take care of my friends who had helped me secure the parts and get the car in top running order.

I wasn't "Louie," but I wanted to live out the theme song popular in those days: "Meet Me in St. Louis." Bettie and I were together for three wonderful days in the city, days that passed all too quickly. When they were over, we promised marriage: Bettie would come out to Denver University to join me when her semester and my quarter ended in June.

From St. Louis, I continued on westward to Denver and arrived there just in time to register and meet my roommate to be, Kaye Thayer. Like me, Kaye was an Air Force veteran who had been living with his family and was eager to get out on his own. We became fast friends and agreed to cast our lot together for a shot at "independent living." We rented a nice basement apartment from an affable older woman only a few miles north of the campus. Because I had a car, we did not have to rely on public transportation and thus could rent decent accommodations outside the campus area. The biggest expense was my phone bill: the telephone company got fat off me for my many Colorado-to-Missouri calls over the next four months. Lucky for me, the bills, which ran well over a hundred dollars per month, were paid for by my savings from the gambling money.

My first quarter in college was a tough one. We had added a third roommate, Joe Guyer, to help pay the rent, and living with a couple of guys who were not exactly the studious type was almost my undoing. Revisiting shades of high school days, Biology 101 nearly became my Alamo. I simply wasn't studying enough outside of classes, nor was I applying good note-taking techniques while in class. This wasn't high school; I had to learn to be a student again.

Twice during our courtship, Bettie and I visited her parents in the little slate mining town of Bangor, Pennsylvania. Bettie had by then cemented relations with her father again, with the unhappy times of the past long forgotten. I found both of her parents to be good, solid people, and they responded to me in a way that made me feel they were pleased that their daughter had finally found the "right man."

Early that June, Bettie and I were married in a simple ceremony in a small Protestant church in Denver, with the minister's wife and small children as witnesses, along with my best man Kaye and with Joe acting as Bettie's "Maid" of Honor. Afterward, our spirited wedding party of four celebrated at the Brown Palace Hotel in downtown Denver well into the morning hours.

twenty-four

New Life

With neither time nor finances to spare for a honeymoon, we newlyweds settled rapidly into a new semester of classes. By this time, the university seemed better prepared to greet the onslaught of veterans and to appreciate the changes they brought to campus. These new students were cut from a different cloth than typical freshmen. Many were already married and had children, others were considerably older and more mature than the college students the universities had known. They were, on average, a deadly serious bunch who had no time for the social niceties of fraternities or sororities and, for the most part, were not impressed with athletics. Eager to get on with their lives, the veterans saw the university degree as a first step toward their goals.

Bettie and I fit this profile to a tee. Overnight, I had become a serious married veteran student with the goal of becoming a writer. The only obstacle at the time was finding housing, which for married students who were veterans was at a premium. Denver University was far behind in erecting semi-permanent housing on campus property, but fortunately for us, federal housing laws were in place that mandated rent controls throughout the country and imposed stiff fines on landlords who exceeded legal requirements in their rental agreements.

Bettie and I rented a small but adequate basement apartment just three blocks from campus. The owner of the house lived next door, and a married couple with their baby lived above us. We felt very lucky to find the unit. With both of us being veterans, we had a combined income of $120 per month, which allowed us to easily pay the rent-controlled payments of $45, including utilities.

We became fast friends with Dick and Mary Lou Barger and baby Ricky who lived in the apartment upstairs, coining our shared landlady as the "Witch of Williams Street." Her name was Hazel, and she had many witchlike attributes, which included being angry and growling all the time about anything that had to do with the property she claimed as "hers." She was primarily out of sorts because she had to rent her two-unit house for so little money "just because of that goddamn government rent control thing." So much for the loyal patriot ready to express gratitude to veterans. She definitely earned being called "Witch Hazel."

During the winter of 1946, Hazel got her revenge on us when the temperature in Northern Colorado, Montana, and Wyoming stayed below freezing for thirty consecutive days, the longest freeze on record. The three states had to use Air Force cargo planes to drop hay bales to the range cattle below; even then, many died by freezing, some in a standing position, before they could be rescued. It was miserable for people like us too, since the only heat for the entire basement apartment was a small, unvented gas heater that barely kept the place warm even in moderately cold weather. Neither Bettie nor I was smart enough to figure out why we started getting severe headaches and were becoming unusually drowsy in the evenings. We had much homework and studying to do each night, but fell asleep with textbooks open across our laps.

One evening, Dick came down to bring us pie that Mary Lou had baked that day. He had been downstairs before but never noticed the little gas heater that was now blazing away constantly for us to stay warm. He sniffed the air a couple times and noticed there wasn't a vent pipe going out through the wall as was required by building codes. Witch Hazel had probably balked at the cost and it was never installed. At Dick's suggestion, we called the fire department the next day. They inspected the gas heater and immediately cited old sourpuss. We two scholars could easily have died in our sleep of carbon monoxide poisoning.

Fortunately, after my marriage to Bettie, and with no outside influences to tempt me, I finally got into the "academic groove." Bettie's courses for the most part paralleled mine, with both of us delving into heavy doses of English as well as early American and world literature. Bettie had also become fascinated with my Greek and Roman classics courses and joined me in a couple the following semester. The competition was good for me; she was, by far, the more diligent student. With her as my study partner, we would prepare for the same tests in our classical studies class and generally ace them the next day. Studying together kept me on my toes and was an entertaining added dimension to the learning process.

Whether it was the military, the marriage, or a combination of the two, I could hardly remember my old self. The boy who had struggled to understand his kindergarten classmates and had literally fought his way through junior high had matured when I wasn't looking.

Eventually word came down that our special veterans housing would be ready in another month. The university had taken on the Herculean task of constructing forty Denver Steel units on a large swath of acreage, with each unit measuring about 850 square feet. Each contained four separate apartments with adjoining common—and very thin—walls. The apartments had two bedrooms, a full but small kitchen with a refrigerator and stove, and a living room that was large enough to include a dining area.

Once again, our veteran status came into play when the university housing priorities were listed with accompanying points: for the number of children the veteran's family had, for the years of service, and for combat decorations. Although we did not have children, our combined years of service and my combat points shot us to the top of the reservation lists.

We were delighted to get out of our burrow on South Williams Street, and old Hazel was not missed. The rent for our new unit was an incredibly low $40 dollars per month, and when I hired on as a part-time worker on the village maintenance crew, I earned enough to satisfy at least half of each month's rent. We even had a little garden plot in the rear of our apartment in which we planted a few veggies. Cultivating just that handful of produce gave us a homesteader feeling.

People were getting on with their lives, and we were inspired to be part of this goal-directed enthusiasm. In our little complex, we had artists majoring in the Fine Arts, business accounting majors, education majors destined to be public school and college teachers, physics and chemistry majors, and engineering majors. We were particularly good friends with another couple like us who had no children. They both majored in archeology, and we spent many weekends outdoors prowling around the mountains, the couple explaining to us various rock formations and the early primitive residents of the area.

We both enjoyed the stimulating environment of the university and I was becoming an even more serious student, spending long hours in the library doing research for term papers and projects. In this atmosphere, I was oblivious to realities of a future outside the college and the military; I had not yet given much thought to how I would support a family, and the GI Bill would be ending soon.

One day, right in the middle of a Shakespeare class, I had a shocking revelation about my plans for the future. I had put writing the Great American Novel on the back burner, and I had to admit to myself that it wasn't just schoolwork that was keeping me from my foggy goal; I feared that when the time came for me to earn a living for my family and there was no more GI Bill, I wouldn't be able to hack the pressure and competition in the publishing world. Sitting down that night with Bettie, I plotted a serious change in my career direction.

The next day, I made an appointment to see the Dean of the

School of Education. While attempting to give him a rationale for changing my major from English to Education, I made the grave mistake of saying that I was doing this primarily because I knew that public school teachers were free during the summer months and that this would give me an excellent opportunity to do my writing for publication. In other words, I planned to use teaching as a "crutch" to earn the steady income that would enable me to support my family and still write during the summer months.

Well, by the time the old dean came off the ceiling and his facial color returned to normal pasty from beet red, he was finally able to sputter out his objection. If I thought I could use teaching "as a crutch," I had better change my mind quickly or there wouldn't be a place for me in his department. Ever.

After attempting to smooth his ruffled feathers, I was finally able to impress him with my grade point average of the first two years, and a promise that I would maintain my record or even better in my future Education courses. He didn't capitulate too easily, warning me that he would pull my records and monitor my classes each term, checking for consistent grades. He vowed passionately that if my grades ever went below a B average, he would personally "send me packing" out of his department. We parted company on that note, and I never saw him again for the rest of my time at the university.

I took to my new major "like a duck to water," completing all required classes in good order and performing my stint of student teaching in a summer session kindergarten. I always wondered if that old dean had been involved in my student teaching assignment, probably thinking I wouldn't do well as a kindergarten teacher. But what an outstanding experience it turned out to be. The five-years-olds—and their parents—were surprised to have a "Mister" teacher, particularly one twice their height. The young ones and I shared a lot besides the required curriculum: watercolor painting, pottery, track runs, geology. We also shared a measure of hyperactivity that helped us all get along. By the end of that quarter, I was convinced that I wanted to become an elementary school teacher when I graduated.

Bettie continued doing well in her classes and I was able to enroll in some of them with her. My future students, I thought, could profit from lessons in Greek and Roman literature. You could tell how little I knew about elementary school curriculum.

Bettie and I had often discussed planning for a child, and we ultimately timed the event for the end of her last quarter of school as if we were ordering a little boy from a Wards catalog (where, by the way, I worked as a part-time clerk in the toy department). This was long before testing could determine the sex of the unborn, but I preemptively bought "him" an electric train set for the Christmas ahead just the same.

Our first-born was indeed the son I had hoped for, but he came nearly three weeks premature. Bettie missed her graduation exercises after an arduous two days of labor and the birth of a six-and-a-half-pound baby boy. We gave him a name respectfully derived from both of our fathers: Brittain Christian. Brittain had to stay in an incubator, but after ten days, we were finally able to bring him home to our little Denver Steel chateau, squawking and fussing about his new surroundings in this strange new world.

That first evening Brittain was home, I suddenly became ill at our dinner table. My stomach pains were so severe that I drove myself to the university clinic. Six hours later, I was rushed by ambulance to Mercy Hospital in Denver with a ruptured appendix. I won't go into the gory details (and gory they were), but I was confined to the hospital for twenty-one days. If it hadn't been for the newly discovered wartime "wonder drug" called penicillin, I wouldn't have been around to share this story with you.

One can imagine the hardship Bettie faced being alone with a tiny newborn and not knowing much about the proper care and feeding of such a little guy. Good fortune was with us once again when my former roommate Kaye and his mother learned of the situation. His mother, who had been a registered nurse for many years, came to the rescue, helping Bettie immeasurably during the three weeks I was hospitalized.

When my health finally returned and I was able to return home, I was twenty pounds lighter and a bit weak, but ready to become a real father and resume my studies during the summer. Having completed the required number of units for my Bachelor's degree, I immediately started on my Master's, working toward a major in Educational Administration. I also began interviewing for a teaching position in the Denver schools, hoping to be hired at the lofty salary of $2,650 a year.

twenty-five

Los Alamos

1949–1955

I was feeling rather liberated as I made my way across the university lawn. After all, I had survived emergency appendectomy surgery, a twenty-one-day hospital stay, a car crash, an encounter with carbon monoxide, and oh yes, thirty-five trips in a B-24. Still, I had only twenty dollars in my wallet. What I needed was a job.

Serendipitously, a fellow student called out to me. "Hey, Jensen, there's a guy over in the placement office, says he's looking for teachers. Some kind of military place... and there's no line."

I rushed to the office to find an imposing six-foot three-inch silver-haired man in full Navy officer's uniform seated behind the desk. Captain F. Robert Wegner Retired was now Superintendent of the Los Alamos School District in Los Alamos, New Mexico. My mind ran rapidly: *Los Alamos—wasn't that the place where they built the atom bomb? They didn't have schools there, did they? This is very strange— a naval officer is the superintendent of schools and he hires teachers?*

After formal introductions, the captain explained theirs was a K–12 district with the finest of government-funded schools, equipment, and curricula. Then we moved on to issues more pertinent to me—salary, housing, moving expenses—and all of his answers pleased me. Most important, I sincerely related to this man. Though we didn't speak in much detail about our wartime life, we each knew the other had had life-changing experiences, and I immediately felt that I could work for and with him comfortably in the years to come.

I learned that the town of Los Alamos was a federal government installation operated and funded by the Atomic Energy Commission (AEC). The Commission's authority was essentially divided into three separate entities, each with its own administration: the Scientific Laboratories were contracted to the University of California; the AEC controlled all community functions and town operations including housing and security; and the ZIA Corporation was a large contracting firm responsible for maintenance of streets and construction of housing and facilities.

The public schools operated independently but were funded entirely by the AEC and were under the general curriculum guidelines of the State of New Mexico. The financial largess bestowed upon the schools by Uncle Sam's AEC enabled the schools to offer a highly enriched program of K–12 public education within modern, quality-built schools that had become the envy of the entire state. In addition to exceptional funding for the schools, the high educational levels of the parents of Los Alamos students meant that nothing but the finest and most progressive form of scholastic programs would be acceptable—and Bob Wegner was just the sort of man to make certain that happened. He had been there only three years, but under his dynamic leadership, the quality of programs and teaching personnel brought statewide recognition.

The prospects sounded great to me. When I shared the news with Bettie, she was also delighted. Bob extended a cordial invitation for both of us to visit him and check out the school system before I signed a contract; all expenses would be paid for the 450-mile trip from Denver. Readily agreeing to his generous offer, we bundled little Britt into the backseat of the Ford coupe and away we went to explore our new community.

From what we could gather, Los Alamos was in transition, with much of its secretiveness already reduced. Dr. Oppenheimer, who had directed the laboratory, had returned to UC Berkeley the prior year, after the first nuclear fusion/atomic bomb was launched. I heard that in earlier years, lab employees were required to change their names and undergo repetitive security clearances, even if their jobs were far from the secrets. No one spelled out the changes to me, but I gathered that the atomic bomb that had been used to halt the war in Japan had been designed and tested right here, with a testing site some 200 hundred miles south.

When we arrived, in the summer of 1949, the entire town of Los Alamos—which included some 12,500 permanent residents residing within a perimeter of over five miles—was enclosed by a ten-foot-high wire mesh fence tipped by additional razor wire. The fence was patrolled by security guards with their dogs on a twenty-four-hour basis. If we moved to Los Alamos, friends and family who planned to visit us from outside the town would need to be "cleared" by the security office at least ten days before being allowed access through the closely guarded main gates. As permanent residents, we would have personal identification cards that would be examined each time we entered or exited the town, and our car would have a coded decal on its windshield allowing its entrance.

Bettie, the baby, and I toured what could be our new home. It was hard to believe that nearly everything—housing, recreational facilities, offices, stores—had been built within the past seven years. It was only in 1942 when General Groves, now the overall project director, found what he considered the ideal site for sensitive research. Both beautiful and remote, the former Boys Prep School was virtually unknown in the state as well as in the country. It had been called by some The Town That Did Not Exist but That Changed the World.

We were completely impressed with the town, the school staff, and the surrounding magnificent beauty of the Jemez Mountains, whose five jutting ridges formed the bases on which the town of Los Alamos was built. The town and the laboratories were on separate plateaus divided by steep canyons at an altitude of 7,250 feet. The complex as a whole had been referred to as "The Hill" ever since the former Los Alamos Boys' Ranch was taken over by the government for the highly secret Manhattan Project, the building of the first atom bomb.

Without a single qualm, I signed on the dotted line for a teaching position that would start in the coming weeks.

Father and Son

Teaching was all and more than I had expected. As a child who struggled for so many years as a student, it was astonishing that I became a teacher. Perhaps my genuine empathy for children who didn't fit the ideal mold guided my choice without realizing it, and I continued on an upward trajectory in the field of education—eventually becoming a principal.

Yes, life was mostly good, but in the days since Kassel, I had striven to find the message in this life after war. The effects of what I went through as an airman never fully left me; although Germany surrendered on May 8, 1945, I still woke nearly every morning thinking of Tibenham. I know I am not alone when I say I did my best to hide the painful and traumatic memories of being in war. I had witnessed planes exploding so close to mine that at times I was flying nearly blind. I had facilitated the death of human beings I didn't—and will never—know. I had lost scores of friends to failed missions. I had experienced multiple near misses, left to wonder why I had been spared.

But when I looked into the eyes of my children—as Papa did mine when I was two, explaining why he was leaving to work on a big ship again, how he'd found a loving caregiver for me in Hamburg, and how he and I would someday go to America—I had my answer.

twenty-six
―

What Became of Us?

I remained in the field of education for my entire career and loved every position I held. Bettie and I had two more children, daughters Dayne and Jarl, making us a family of five. Through a series of troubling circumstances, ours was not to be a lifelong relationship, but in the twenty-one years that Bettie and I were together, our children benefited greatly from her guidance. Happily, I did find love again years later, when I met and married my loving wife, Mary. We had more than forty years together and enjoyed extensive travels, which was something we had both always wanted to do. Mary chronicled these sometimes quirky trips in an award-winning book called *Rudy's Rules for Travel*.

As for my family of heritage, all of our lives were impacted by the war, but Papa seemed to change the most. He was no longer the bombastic German loyalist. He studied photos of concentration camps and saw firsthand, in the streets of DC, wounded survivors of the war's destruction. He grew more and more withdrawn, sitting in his chair with newspapers strung across his lap as he absorbed the truth about the horrors of the Nazi regime. Of course Papa never verbally admitted he had been wrong, but his suffering was evident.

Sending emergency packages to German families was probably Papa's most healing activity. Despite the poverty he and Mutti endured, he led a veritable assembly-line factory in our apartment along with Mutti, Uncle Carl, and Aunt Nettel for three years, sending hundreds of boxes to Hamburg, Dresden, and the villages. They even packed boxes for the Frau and Herta, the Jewish mother and daughter who took care of me in Hamburg, but the two were never found.

I helped my family when I visited home, filling the heavier boxes and carrying them to the post office. The irony and tragedy wasn't lost on me: I, who had destroyed life, was now attempting to patch it back together.

Out of necessity, Papa worked as a waiter as long as he physically could. Mutti continued to financially support him, and they remained in the little apartment in DC. Even though it was a slow conversion, Papa finally became an American citizen in the 1950s.

As soon as Germany occupied Czechoslovakia, Uncle Carl, the butler at the Czech embassy in DC, had been directed to raise the German—that is, Nazi—flag. He was distressed when his picture appeared on the front page of the local and national papers. Years later, on the day Germany signed its surrender, Carl proudly raised the Czech flag again. When he and Aunt Nettel retired, the family for whom they had worked gifted them vacant land, a part of which is now Tyson Corners just outside the city. Carl took night school classes to earn a realtor's license. The couple soon became American citizens and examples of the promise of immigration.

Henri Hirsch, the gentleman I visited as a child in New York City, accepted a visit from Papa. I learned from Mutti that Papa had packed a small worn case and boarded the morning train. Mutti knew only that he needed "to beg forgiveness" before Henri, who was near the end of his life, passed away. As it turned out, Papa was also near the end of his. Returning home, Papa said that he was now free to die, that Mr. Hirsch had forgiven him. Not long after, Papa succumbed to heart failure. We are left to wonder exactly what was forgiven.

Jimmy and Jesse were my closest friends since adolescence. Sadly, Jesse was killed in the war, but Jimmy and I communicated nearly every month after it ended, writing or calling each other for nearly seventy years. Every so often I traveled to DC so that Jimmy and I could ride through the old neighborhoods, sharing stories with current residents and any passersby who would listen.

Anna Weber, my Mutti, had envisioned a new life in America as a young woman, but that was not what she found. She and Papa, after all those years of working, barely had enough to pay for their funeral plot. Nonetheless, she was a resilient woman, grateful to have lived outside the World War II combat zones. She was forever thankful to have her son safely returned to her, and, despite their difficulties, to grow in affection for Papa. She became an American citizen as well.

Father and Son

After Papa died, Carl and Nettel sold some of their land, enough to buy a bungalow for Mutti near the shore in Florida, right next to their new house. I was stricken when I heard she had been diagnosed with cancer, a disease less common in those days. Sadly, Mutti died just before moving in. Nettel was somewhat comforted by the knowledge that Mutti knew she finally had a home to call her own.

Papa's knapsack, slung over his shoulder, had gone everywhere with him since he was fourteen years old and started working for the Hamburg American liner. For fifty years that knapsack accompanied him from port to port, apartment to apartment. After Papa's death, I was helping Mutti sort Papa's meager belongings when I came upon the knapsack. It contained the answers to the questions I had long harbored: *During all those years I waited for you, Papa, waited for the gulf between us to close, did you think about me? Did you love me?*

With the exceptions of a stray comb, coin purse, and a little book of German poetry, the knapsack contained mostly photos of me. A typical portrait of an infant on a bear rug. As a toddler with a life-sized stuffed white rabbit. As a child with a very much alive companion and guard dog. A tiny sailor practicing his salute. A young man in dress military uniform.

Each photo was securely wrapped, backed in cardboard, and covered in sturdy brown wax brown paper. Papa had collected, carried, and guarded these photos for forty years.

I knew now—he had always loved me.

Afterword

I thumbed through the mail that day, catalogues and bills offering distraction in equal measure. Anything seemed better than facing again the questions that rose each time I studied Rudy's writings. As an editor, it was my job to introduce him to you as he was, particularly as he was in his relationship with his father and the constantly changing American landscape behind his life.

I had lived with Rudy nearly forty years. I had heard four decades of stories about his childhood during the Great Depression, being an Enemy Alien during World War II, and fighting his land of birth. Most of all I had learned about how it was to live with Papa, for Papa dominated life. But just who was this man?

One morning, several years after Rudy's death, the mail brought another clue. I opened a thin catalogue to a page promoting a newly released book, Rhodri Jeffrey Jones' *The Nazi Spy Ring in America*. Early in his text, Jones focuses on the shipping and passenger liner, the Hamburg America, the line that Papa and his father before him called home while its ships sailed between New York and Hamburg. Jones accuses the line's executives and captains of facilitating connections between Nazi spies of varying echelons as they carried documents, technology blueprints, maps, and individuals between the two countries.

Papa was virtually raised on ships of the line, from the age of sixteen until he left to take up residence in America and to work as a head waiter to Washington's elite. That elite eventually included J. Edgar Hoover. It raised the questions: Just how does a German-born waiter get his first job in America in a prestigious hotel in Washington frequented by leading senators and cabinet members? What was the necessity for the family to frequently change apartments? And when his family apartment was raided by the FBI at the entry of America into World War II, why were only his wife and teenaged son named Enemy Aliens?

We—and perhaps you—would say that Papa was far too outspoken an advocate of Nazi Germany to ever become a discreet spy. He sang German opera from the apartment balcony, had weekly dinners for German friends, and never kept a thought to himself.

In one typical conversation, Rudy and I went round and round the same questions. I usually opened the debate with, "Well, was your Papa a spy for Germany planted to be near J. Edgar Hoover? To overhear the agency's work of the day? And what about his boisterous outbursts? He seemed to never stop talking in defense of Germany, carrying on about how they were so mistreated after World War I."

"Exactly," Rudy typically replied. "What better cover?"

Remembering his 300-pound, six-foot-three frame, I finally dared ask: "Was he J. Edgar's bodyguard? Or friend? Or ...?"

Rudy shrugged. "We'll never know."

As a final note, I also find it curious that Henri Hirsch made a special effort to invite Rudy to New York and to make such a fuss over him, even introducing him to all of his friends. Is it possible that Henri was more to Rudy than we knew?

A Memorial

Photo credit: Kassel Mission Historical Society, www.kasselmission.org

After the war, a memorial was erected in a glade just outside the little German village of Friedlos where American B-24s and German fighter planes fell the day of the Kassel Raid. A small cemetery still contains the graves of some of the Americans and Germans who died there. A bronze plaque describes the battle while smaller rocks stand to each side of the main memorial stone, bearing the names of Americans and Germans killed on this tragic day. An active Kassel Mission Memorial Association (KMMA.org) has a large membership of both Germans and Americans, some of whom meet annually in different cities of America or in Germany.

Like most European babies, I posed au naturel

With my guardian, Benno

My caregivers Frau Hauenbarger, Herta, and Papa

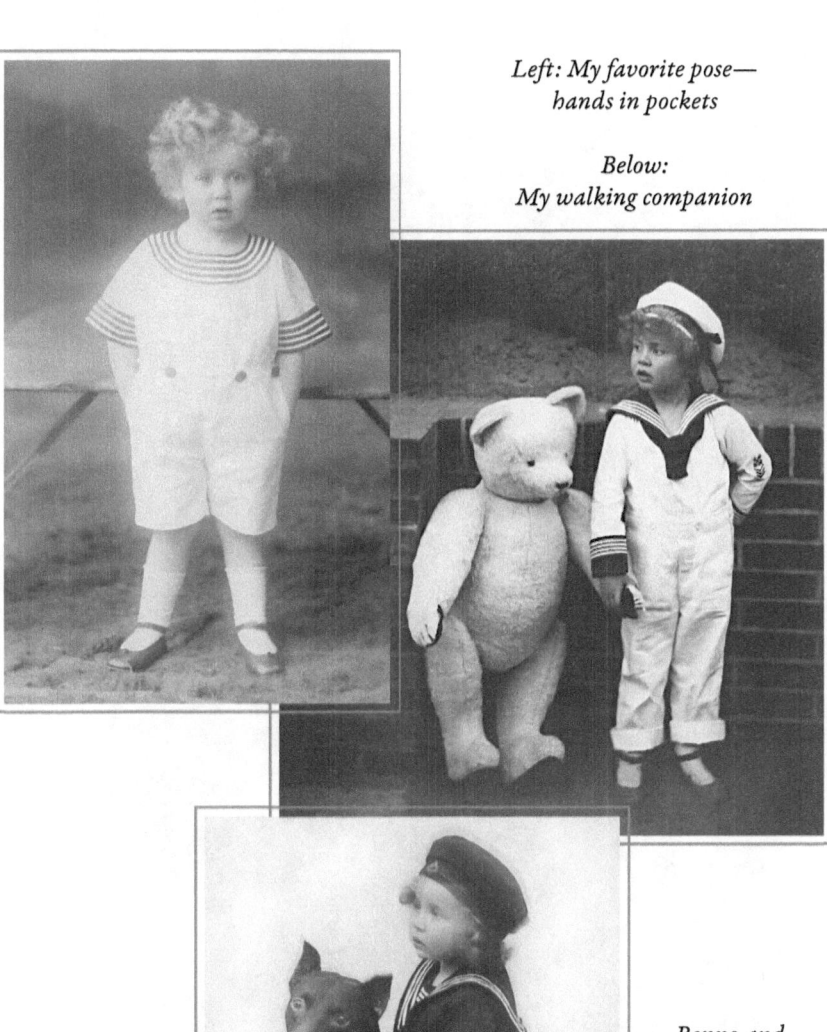

Left: My favorite pose—hands in pockets

Below: My walking companion

Benno and I grow up a bit

Papa in New York City in the 20s

*Grandfather Simon
Christian Johannes Jensen*

*Grandmother with her second
husband, Herman Seifert*

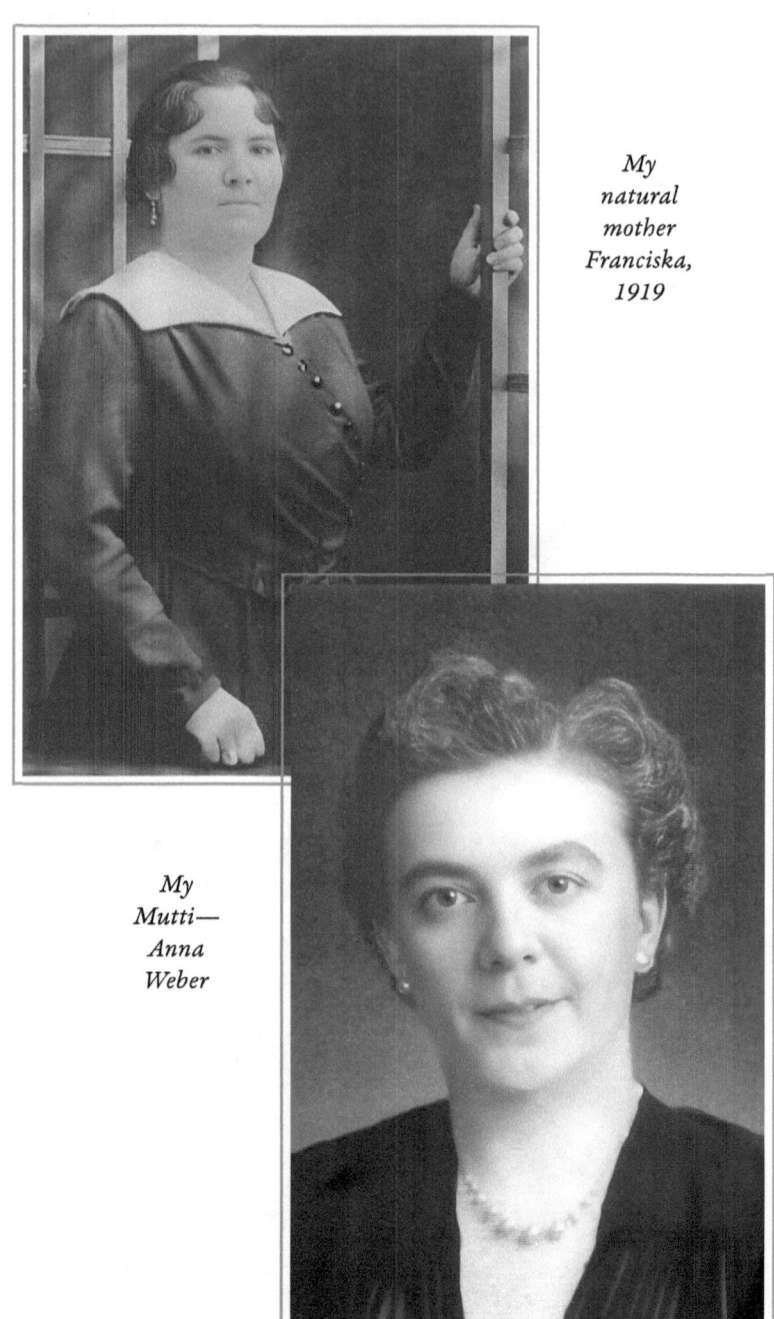

My natural mother Franciska, 1919

My Mutti— Anna Weber

High school graduation, 1941

I was a citizen, at last!

Joining the US Army Air Force

Training for a B-24 waist gunner position

Our crew, grateful we survived together

Recreation time on our only vehicles

Home sweet home

Our B24 drops back to its target

I painted nose art for our first plane.

Photo from the Rudy Jensen Collection MC376/8. Norfolk Record Office, American Library Memorial to the 2nd Air Division, 8th Air Force, United States Army Air Forces Norfolk and Norwich Millennium Library, Norfolk, UK.

Waist gunner position

My first teacher photo at Los Alamos

Bettie

Brittain

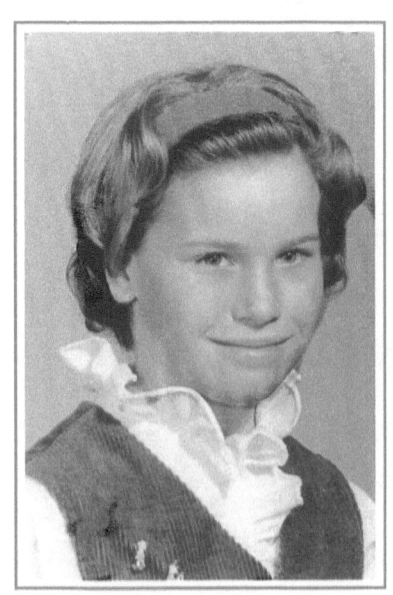

Dayne

Jarl

As principal of my first school

Nettel (left) and Mary

*Local leaders welcome me back to Tibenham.
On my right, Richard Bacon, member of Parliament;
on my left, Evan Harris, chair of Norfolk Gliding Club.*

Last flying B24 visits Chico, CA

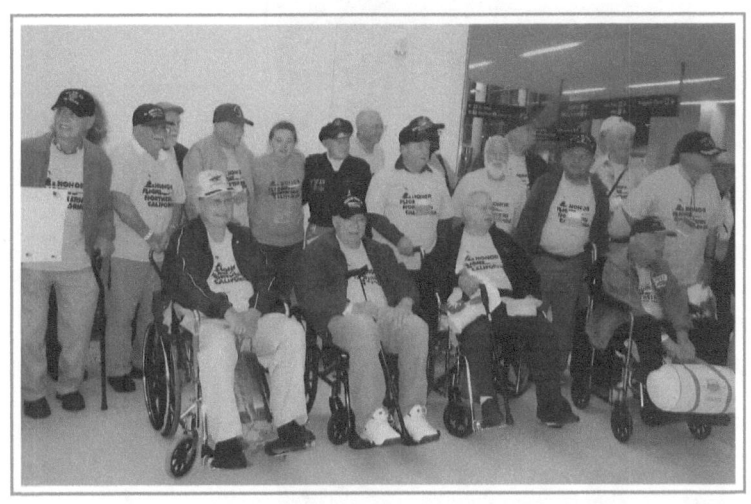

A gathering of veterans

DC Memorial to WWII

Partners in war

I have often visited my mentor, Abraham

Rudy was fond of building model ships . . .

. . . and of painting in watercolor
(This is only one of many beautiful paintings
Rudy did in his retirement years)

Acknowledgments

I first knew the work of Stacey Aaronson, of The Book Doctor Is In, when she designed the book I had written for She Writes Press. I was impressed then with her ability to capture my intent and spirit as a writer. In producing this book, my admiration for her continued to grow. A gifted writer and editor, she has also been an encouraging guide, and focused producer. It is no exaggeration to say that Rudy's work found here would not exist without her.

Family and friends have been ceaseless in their interest and support. Two have, with me, been a team dedicated to telling the stories of Rudy's generation. Anne Russell was our initial editor and David York our photographer. Both are talented artists and technicians. I am grateful to Kiersten Norris who shepherded the manuscript through its early versions and to my writing group who never lost faith.

About the Authors

RUDOLF (RUDY) JENSEN earned his Masters degree in educational administration at Denver University under the GI bill after World War II. His interest in education began when, as a student teacher, he was assigned a kindergarten class. He found that he and the five-year-olds had much in common—a love of nature and a certain level of hyperactivity. After forty years of working in the California and Los Alamos schools, Rudy was selected as a student trainee evaluator at California State University Chico, a position he held for several years before his death. His retirement years lent him opportunity to develop talents in watercolor, woodworking, and travel.

MARY K. JENSEN earned her PhD at the University of Oregon where she was an analyst and writer for their federal research clearinghouse. Prior to her doctoral training, she worked at CSU Chico and in California schools, in an array of roles: teaching, school psychology, and administration. She is a member of California Writers Club and is published in North State Writers' 2017 and 2024 anthologies. Mary lives in northern California where she relishes her writing group, book clubs, and friendships. Her recent book, *Rudy's Rules for Travel: Life Lessons from around the Globe*, shows another side of Rudy you won't want to miss. www.marykjensen.com

Available at all major online retailers

2019 IPPY Silver Medal Winner in Travel - Essay

2019 Kirkus Reviews, named a Best Book of the Year

2019 Independent Book Publishers Association Gold Medalist in Travel

2019 Independent Book Publishers Association,
Silver Medalist in Memoir

2019 Independent Book Publishers Awards Silver Medalist in Travel

2019 Next Generation Indie Book Awards:
Finalist in Travel/Travel Guide

2019 Next Generation Indie Book Awards: Finalist in Memoir (Other)

2019 Foreword Indies Finalist in Adult Nonfiction—Travel

2019 IBPA Ben Franklin Awards Finalist in Travel

"A set of rules for life, by way of a delightful travel narrative.... A book that will make readers want to pack their bags and catch the first flight to somewhere far away."

—*Kirkus Reviews*, starred review

"Traveling with Rudy was not easy. The school principal and WWII veteran was determined to stretch every dollar to its limit, meet the locals, and get off the beaten tourist path, as his long-suffering wife attests in this fun and tender memoir. From exotic destinations like Bali to more personal excursions to uncover family history, Rudy's travels are imbued with his unceasing optimism and boundless enthusiasm, leaving the reader convinced that his rules are well worth following."

—*Booklist*

"Armchair travelers and their active counterparts, spouses who have traveled or are thinking of traveling together, solo trekkers, women journeyers, and dysfunctional spouses will enjoy this work."

—*Library Journal Xpress*

www.ingramcontent.com/pod-product-compliance
Lightning Source LLC
Chambersburg PA
CBHW020527080526
44583CB00013B/764